The Windermere Ferry

HISTORY, BOATS, FERRYMEN AND PASSENGERS

Dick White

With acknowledgement to the assistance of
the Curwen Archive Trust

HELM
PRESS

Dedicated to The Windermere Ferrymen

Published by Helm Press
10 Abbey Gardens, Natland, Kendal, Cumbria LA9 7SP
Tel: 015395 61321
E-mail: HelmPress@natland.freeserve.co.uk

First published 2002

Typeset in Bembo and Lucida Sans

ISBN 0 9540497 1 3

Typeset and printed by
Miller Turner Printers, The Sidings, Beezon Fields, Kendal Cumbria LA9 6BL

Front cover: John Eric Atkinson (Johnnie) photograph gifted to him with compliments
and thanks Joseph Hardman, 3 Park Avenue, Kendal – January 1938
Back Cover:
Top: Pre 1870 Ferry loading at Ferry House, the late Charlotte Kipling
Bottom: 1915 Steam Ferry - Atkinson & Pollit, The 'Drake' 1954, The 'Mallard' 1990

CONTENTS

Etching of Windermere Lake, from the Ferry House.
T Allom and W Taylor

FOREWORD

This is the fascinating story - sometimes exciting, occasionally tragic - of the Windermere Ferry which, for many hundreds of years, in its different forms, has been carrying passengers, vehicles and animals across England's largest lake. The tale, meticulously researched over many years, has been compiled by a Cumbrian born scientist, Dick White, now living near Lancaster, who for some years, worked for the Freshwater Biological Association at Ferry House, a few yards away from the ferry landing, and who for several years used the boat daily.

Mr White has managed to incorporate almost every known fact about the ferry – its long history, the different boats beginning with the earliest rowed craft, the owners, the ferrymen and the passengers – producing a lively addition to a piece of little-known Lake District history. As an example of his thorough research he provides the names and some of the addresses of all the forty-eight passengers who, with seven horses, were drowned when the Ferry, laden with a large party returning from a Hawkshead Market and wedding in October 1635, foundered in the lake.

I have known the Ferry, and several of its ferrymen, for much of a long life and have often written about it in my books or articles while my memories of Windermere go back to the Great Freeze of 1929 when I skated, completely on my own, for two or three miles up the lake, leaving the massed crowds – and many cars – packed on the ice at Lakeside, enjoying the rare winter carnival. May I commend this entertaining history as a rewarding read.

A. Harry Griffin M.B.E.
February 2002

INTRODUCTION

I was born at Cumwhinton, near Carlisle in 1934. My father was in the bank and we moved frequently, first to Maryport but then in 1946 to Windermere, where I went to school. In 1951 I started work for the Freshwater Biological Association based at Ferry House across the lake, and a few yards from the western Ferry landing. This entailed making the journey backwards and forwards over the lake on each working day. I left Ferry House in 1958 and went to work in London, where I developed my career as a microbiologist. However, my journeys on the Ferry had left me with an abiding interest in the old Ferry boat.

When the ferry boat 'Drake' was replaced in 1990 by the new boat 'Mallard', I fell to wondering about the service and its history. I realised I knew little of events concerning it, and set about collecting information. Apart from Bruce Thompson's antiquarian essay, published in 1971, there is nothing of a comprehensive nature, and this book is an attempt to draw the facts together in one place. Much of the information is widely scattered, often existing in private collections, personal memories and obscure sources. I have quoted some passages at length to give readers a taste of the times (or perhaps to help if they wish to retrace my steps). I have, during my twelve years of research, enjoyed collecting prints, paintings, drawings, postcards, photographs and other illustrations to share with you in my quest to capture as much of the life and times of the Ferry as possible, together with the people, ferrymen and the interesting and amusing anecdotes I could collect along the way.

William White from 'Furness Folk and Facts'.

A further impetus to my study came when I found that a William White, to whom I believe I am distantly related, and who was the last of the shipbuilders

Dick at Ferry House in the 1950s.

on the Ulverston Canal, built a ferry for Windermere in 1872. It was built in Ulverston and conveyed on a wagon drawn by horses to Newby Bridge at the foot of the lake where it was launched.

I do not claim this to be the whole story, and indeed one of the objectives in producing the book is to identify areas of doubt, error and omission in the hope others may know additional details and contact me to add to the story. I have made every effort to be sure my information is as accurate and correct as possible, and would be grateful for notification of corrections to incorporate in future editions.

I am indebted to the great number of people who have so unstintingly helped me along the way and I am extremely grateful for their time and energy: among them are the County Record Offices in Preston, Kendal, Whitehaven and Carlisle; Public Libraries in Carlisle, Barrow, Ulverston, Kendal and Windermere; and the Armitt Library in

Ambleside. Many individuals have given me assistance including: Joyce Hewkin, Kathleen Atkinson, the late Eric Clark, Cliff Atkinson, the late David Brayshaw, Diana Matthews, Bruce Logan, Anne Colville, Mike Smith, Harold Gidman, Bryan Walker, Bill Perry, Geoff Phillips, Eric Dobson, Bob Crowther, Jack Little, John Norton, Roger Quartermaine, Mike Nield, Phillip Bonney, Michael Rutter, Jenifer Borer, Sylvia Harrison, the late Harry Byers, Barry Croft, Colin Tyson, the late Charlotte Kipling, Bill Oughted, Hilary Ainsworth, John Williams, John Marsh and Percy Duff.

I was fortunate to meet the late Eric Clark of Cunsey while researching the Ferry. Eric was ferryman John Atkinson's son-in-law, and he generously gave me a collection of photographs, some of which are reproduced in this book.

My wife, Pamela, has encouraged, helped and tolerated, in addition to reading and rereading the manuscript. Anne Bonney has been a much-appreciated mentor and has instilled some semblance of

The late Eric Clark

order into my haphazard collection of information. I thank them all for their valuable contributions.

I hope you will now read on and enjoy the Windermere Ferry, its history, its people and characters through the years, set on and around one of the most beautiful lakes in the country. Perhaps, if you have not done so already, you will wish to partake of that journey across Windermere that I one time took pleasure in daily.

Dick White

Dick White, The Barn, Stodday, Lancaster LA2 0AG.
Tel: 01524 64314
January 2002

Chapter One
WINDERMERE

As the largest lake in England, Windermere is well known to many people. It is some ten and a half miles long (17km), almost a mile wide (1.4km) at its broadest, 217 feet deep (64m) at its greatest depth and containing 69.3 billion gallons (315 million cu.m.) of water.

The lake was formed following the great ice age when dams of clay and drift material were left in the valley floors allowing water to accumulate. Windermere is made up of two deep sections, known as the north and south basins, joined by a shallow middle region marked by numerous islands, near Bowness. The name Windermere is derived from old Scandinavian meaning 'lake of a man called Vinandr.' By the 12th century it had become Winandermere and more recently Windermere. Nationally the water is known as Lake Windermere, but local people call it simply Windermere since the ending 'mere' means lake. The nearby town of Windermere took its name from the lake when it grew to become a substantial community following the coming of the railway in 1847. Using the name Lake Windermere betrays you as an off comer.

For early travellers the lake created a barrier between the old market towns of Kendal and Hawkshead, and those wishing to go directly between them would have had a detour adding several miles to their journey by having to travel around the head or foot of the lake. A ferry at the central point is clearly of great assistance to such folk.

The origins of a ferry crossing at this central point are unclear. That the Romans used the lake for transporting goods is known from the presence of a quay at Galava Camp on the River Rothay at the head of the lake near Ambleside. The late William Rollinson, a noted local historian indicated probable Roman roads running from Watercrook, near Kendal, to Galava and on to Hardknott Fort on the way to Ravenglass on the Solway Coast. In the absence of evidence for significant traffic going from Kendal to Hawkshead it seems unlikely that a regular cross-

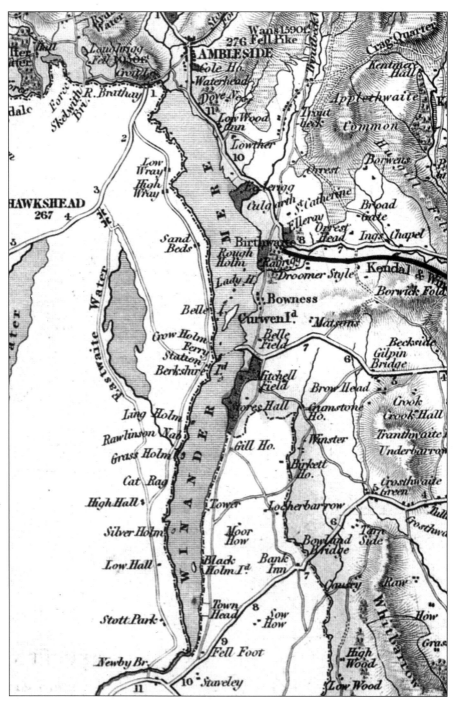

Map of Windermere from Westmorland Map by J & C Walker, of 1830 with later addition of railway.

Old Ferry House, Millerground.   *John Marsh Collection*

lake service in the central part would have been needed at that time. However, no doubt the sheltered havens of Ash Landing and Mitchell's Wyke could have been used in Roman times to load and unload goods.

The next influential residents, who may have had an interest in providing a regular cross-lake service at the central convenient crossing point, were the monastic communities, which flourished from the 12th century. St Mary's Abbey of Furness was founded in 1127, and the monks soon owned all the land between the eastern shore of Coniston Water and the western shore of Windermere. The ability to cross conveniently to markets, and communicate with other communities could have been a stimulus for establishing a ferry. That the monks used Windermere for fishing and for transporting goods is clear from documentary evidence. In 1246 a grant was made to the Abbey of Furness permitting the monks to have a boat on Windermere 'to carry wood and timber and whatever else they need.' They were also allowed to keep a boat for fishing. Documentary evidence for the existence of boats carrying goods on the lake thus starts in the 13th century.

The location of the present service is an obvious place for a ferry. It is near the mid-point of the lake, saving several miles over the journey round the head or bottom of Windermere, and is almost in a direct line between the important towns of Kendal and Hawkshead. The lake narrows to near five hundred metres, due to the presence of promontories

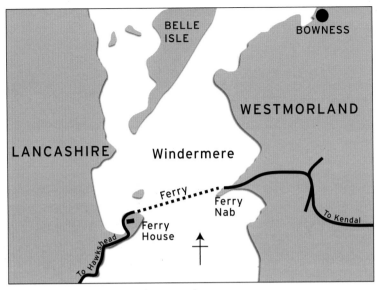

Ferry Nab to Ferry House (Ferry Inn)

sticking out opposite each other from the eastern and western shores. It gives easy access to those working or holidaying in the nearby settlements of Bowness and Windermere to the Furness hinterland. In several early references the crossing at this point is called the 'Horse Ferry', presumably because it was where horses could be conveyed across the lake.

Other freight and passenger carrying boats also used the lake. It must have been much the easiest means of transporting goods before the road infrastructure was properly developed. Slate, charcoal, iron ore and other bulk loads could be shipped along the lake more easily than being transported by pack horse or cart. Passenger services, as represented by the present day steamers, were also well-known.

Two minor ferry crossings are recorded. One at Lakeside at the south or bottom end of the lake, and another from Millerground to Belle Grange towards the middle of the north basin. There is little documentary or other evidence about these ferries. It is assumed they used small rowing boats, and transported only people.

The so-called Horse Ferry, the subject of this book appears to be the principal cross-lake service. Travellers of all kinds have used it. In the earliest times they would have been principally merchants, farmers, peddlers and artisans, using the crossing to help their commercial activities. Later, from the end of the 18th century there were increasing numbers of tourists, enjoying the scenery and homely Lake District hospitality.

Chapter Two
THE FERRY BOATS

There are no descriptions of the earliest rowed boats, but in the 18th century a number of prints and paintings show the kind of boat then in use. In the 19th century, with the advent of a steam ferry and photography, both detailed technical descriptions and clear reliable images became available. By the time of the second steam ferry in 1915, accurate technical specifications can be consulted, and personal recollections accessed.

THE ROWED FERRIES

The earliest references to the boats relate to ownership of the rights of ferriage, the rents and fees payable, and only occasionally the vessels themselves. In 1575 it is documented that the Ferry was allowed to transport horses and men. This indicates the boat must have been of sufficient size to accommodate a large load. In 1635 the occurrence of an accident in which some forty-eight people and seven horses are reputed to have drowned is recorded. Such a cargo indicates a boat of considerable size, probably well in excess of ten metres in length, and of adequate beam. The likelihood is that the boats would have been flat-bottomed to allow reliable grounding at the landings.

One of the earliest illustrations, a print of 1792, shows a clinker built vessel, but most later illustrations show carvel built hulls.

An article of agreement dated 1699 between Miles Sandys of Graythwaite and others, records that Thomas Braithwaite had lately built a new ferry boat. Another document dated 1707 notes the transfer of two ferry boats between ferrymen. The boats appeared in most cases to be driven by two oars (or sweeps) often shown amidships, the sweeps appearing to be as long as the boat. It may have required two men per sweep to manage the boat in rough conditions. Passengers are likely to have had to give assistance. The crossing time was probably twenty to

Print of 1792 showing clinker built vessel. Drawn from nature by W Burgess and engraved by F Dukes.

Old ferry boat landing at Ferry Nab.

John Marsh Collection

thirty minutes but it would have varied greatly, depending on wind direction and strength, and on the load. Some carriages would have influenced the surface area exposed to the wind, which would have affected the boat's progress. A stern load-

'Mary Anne' the preserved old ferry boat at the Windermere Steamboat Museum.

ing ramp is clearly shown in several images.

The remains of one of the rowed ferries is sunk in Mitchell Wyke behind Ferry House. Another is the 'Mary Anne' preserved at the Windermere Steamboat Museum. This boat's dimensions are 10m long by 3.5m broad, and 1m deep.

While some artists have portrayed a ferry under sail, it seems most unlikely that this method of propulsion could have been used success-fully. The artists may have mistakenly believed that sailing boats they saw at the Ferry Inn were the ferry, when they were more likely to have been delivering cargo up and down the lake.

Sailing barge with load on upper lake late 18th early 19th century.

Pre 1870 ferry loading at Ferry House.
The late Charlotte Kipling

Pre 1870 ferry leaving Ferry Nab side.   *The late Charlotte Kipling*

1870 'THE FIRST STEAM FERRY'

In 1870 the Curwen family of Belle Isle owned the ferry rights, and a new steam ferry commenced operation. An account in the Westmorland Gazette for 12th November 1870 reported as follows:

'This beautiful but hitherto inconvenient crossing place on Windermere Lake has now been greatly changed for the better. The steamer and chains, which have taken the place of the old lumbering row boat, complete the crossing and return in much less time than the old boat took to go one way. The men employed are also prompt and obliging, so much so that they hurry across the lake on hearing the first intimation of a passenger. On several occasions we are informed a lusty 'old owl' has called the boat across late on in the night.'

George Pattinson, in his book 'The Great Age of Steam on Windermere' gives an account of the new boat.

'The design and construction of the new steam ferry, which must have been quite a novelty at the time, was supervised by an engineer, George Dixon of Balla Wray. The boiler and engine were on the same side, causing a list to one side, and barrels had to be lashed to the opposite side to counteract this. Later these were removed, and the ballast was put inside the hull. The ferry's steam engine was used, not to drive paddles or a propeller, but to haul the boat across

17

Stengel postcard showing the lopsided first steam ferry.

*the lake by means of a chain around the winding wheel. The chain was even-
tually replaced by a wire rope, but this alone was not entirely satisfactory, as on
two occasions it snapped. In one case the ferry drifted on to Rampholme, near
Storrs, and the other time it floated as far as Belle Isle; after this an additional
guide rope was added for safety.'*

Postcards and photographs of this ferry showed it to have three large
driving wheels on the 'up lake' side, though these are not commonly
seen since most pictures seem to have been taken from the 'down lake'
side. The wire cables, one each side and firmly attached on each shore
were of about 2.5cm diameter. The driving mechanism consisted of
winding wheels around which the cable was looped. There was sufficient slack in the cable to allow it to lie on the lake bed when not in use
and to drop steeply away in front and behind the boat so that the risk of
passing boats catching it was minimal. Early pictures also show a dinghy
suspended from davits, and an anchor. Presumably these were necessary
in view of its habit of breaking loose. The boiler and engine were originally uncovered, but later a shed arrangement is seen covering them
and probably also providing shelter for the ferrymen. Bruce Thompson
records that:

*'It was possible to carry a coach-and-four, or two coaches if the leaders were
detached. Rigg's Coniston Coach made the crossing every weekday in summer,
and the Hawkshead carrier's hooped carts three times a week on their way to
and from Kendal.'*

1870 Ferry as originally commissioned taken by Frith's. Coach and four on left has Furness Abbey on side. Note the anchor on far right.

1870 Steam Ferry at Ferry House note the three large driving wheels.

There is something of a mystery about the identity of the boat's design-er, George Dixon of Balla Wray. The Dixon family lived at Balla Wray House in 1870. They had business interests in the North-East, and the house was used for holidays. Father of the family was Jeremiah Dixon, and there were three sons and two daughters. (An earlier Jeremiah was an astronomer and surveyor who gave his name to the Mason Dixon Line in North America. The song 'I wish I was in Dixie' derives from this geographical feature). John, the eldest son was an engineer, and was known for having brought back Cleopatra's Needle from Egypt. Raylton was a shipbuilder, and Waynman another engineer. The family had all the expertise necessary for designing a ferry, but the identity of George is unclear. He may have been a relative who used the family's knowledge to devise a steam ferry. A letter in the Westmorland Gazette for 30th January 1915 about the introduction of the new steam ferry complicates the story even more:

> 'Sir, - In crossing with the old ferry, in its senile days, I thought I caught a snatch of its soliloquy[1], which its able literary administrator must have missed. To the best of my recollection, it ran thus:

1 Soliloquy - talking to oneself.

My six and forty years of running,
Attest the engineering cunning
And genius of that master mind,
By which I was at first designed
His was the Herculean fame,
Of bringing to the banks of Thame,
That mighty monolith we see,
Raised to the Queen of Antony.

With apologies, - I am etc. Geo. Dixon, Howe End, Far Sawrey.'

The reference to Cleopatra's Needle implies that John Dixon designed the boat. The George Dixon of Howe End has not been identified. Long-term residents of Sawrey are unable to recall such a person, though he is shown to be at that address in a Directory of 1911.

By the end of its life, the first steam ferry had gained an unenviable reputation for being slow, unreliable and inadequate. Barry Croft, of Bowness recalled his grandfather telling of going over on the boat when the ferryman dropped pieces of paper in the water to see which way it was going. They had nearly reached the otherside when the ferryman decided to go back to pick up another passenger. The crossing took the best part of an hour.

Awaiting the early Ferry.

Busy scene at Ferry Nab. The sender who wrote this on 11th June 1905 – 'Arrived here last night. Rather hard work from Kirkby Lonsdale. The scenery is beautiful this time of year. Going to Keswick this afternoon.'

Turn of the century post card – note disconnected pair of horses in second carriage to allow all to get on board at Ferry Nab.

Pretty scene with lady on the left fishing and the ferry going across with work horses and cart loaded with goods.

The 'Here and There' column of the Westmorland Gazette for 9th January 1915 contained the following comment:

'The old ferryboat on Windermere, chiefly remarkable for the lustre of its fittings and the lopsidedness of its gait is about to be superannuated. No one within living memory has done full justice to that ferryboat. Charles Lamb[1] died an age too soon. His genius would have been almost equal to the task. His impressions of the Windermere Ferry composed in the vein in which he celebrated the Old South Sea House, would have done something to redress the rudeness and contumely with which the ancient vessel had been spoken of in a perverse and bustling generation. Has it not been actually suggested that the lake at Ferry Nab should be bridged? The author of that notion would probably be willing to abolish Charon and bridge the Styx. Is it not told that on one evening each year, near the summer solstice, as the skipper of the Ferry makes his last journey for the day from the Westmorland to the Lancashire shore, an ancient dame hurries down to the waters edge on foot, scans the advancing vessel as if intending to board it, shudders, hides her face in her hands, exclaims "Nay, I canna, it's nivver a boat, it's a conundrum" and vanishes in the dusk - until the next season? Well she and the famous boat have grown old and fabulous together - how old, no one unaided by inspiration can tell. And if it is indeed true that a new and well founded vessel is to take the place of the old, despised and rejected machine, one cannot but wonder what will become of the lady.'

1 Charles Lamb was an English essayist who was active at the beginning of the 19th century.

Ferry boat (pre 1915) mid lake loaded with horses and carts.   *Late Eric Clark*

Cliff Atkinson of
Sawrey with the anchor
from the 1870 ferry in
January 2002.

1915 THE SECOND STEAM FERRY

By the time of the First World War, the first steam ferry was showing its age. A combination of mechanical unreliability, inadequate capacity and technological progress made its replacement inevitable. Mr Bruce Logan, lessee of the Ferry House and tenant of the ferry rights, put in hand the building of a new ferry boat. George Pattinson records that the boat was built at Ferry Nab by workmen brought down from Scotland.

> 'These men found it difficult to keep away from the inns at Bowness, and were often absent for two or three days a week until their money had gone. It may have been because of these habits that the boat accidentally launched itself. It almost reached Belle Isle before it was arrested and towed back for completion. Once properly commissioned the new ferry sailed alongside the old ferry for a while, until her owners were satisfied that she was quite safe and not a danger to the public.'

Indeed there is a photograph in the Kendal Public Library showing the two boats side by side in the middle of the lake. Quite how this was arranged is a mystery since both boats would have needed guide and driving cables, presumably anchored at the landings. The risk of fouled cables and a serious accident seem obvious.

The two ferries side by side, 1870 ferry on the left and new version on the right.
Local Studies Section, Kendal Library

1915 Ferry with two ferry men aboard.   *Late Eric Clark*

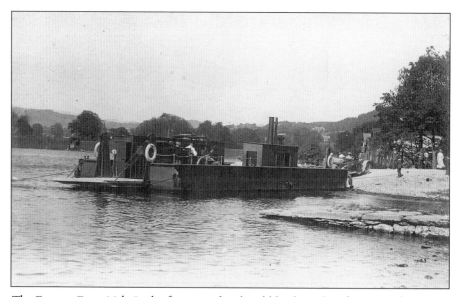

The Ferry at Ferry Nab. In the foreground is the old landing place for rowed ferries and behind this can be seen Walker's Boat Yard.

Yeomanry leaving the Ferry in the 1914-18 War, during manoeuvres. Taken by Herbert & Sons, Windermere.
Late Eric Clark

Atkinson and Pollitt, of Kendal, photograph showing the ferry leaving Ferry House side in the 1920s and the two ferry cables are clearly seen.

Plan of the 1915 Ferry
County Record Office, Kendal

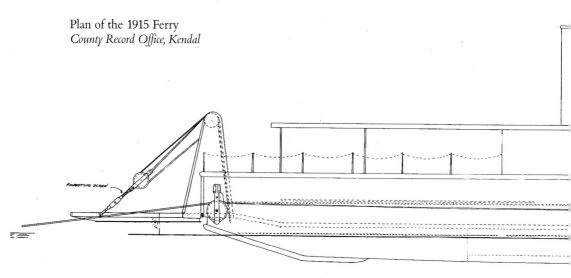

NOTE: WHEN PLATFORMS ARE LEVEL & THE FULL LOAD
OF 8 TONS IS ON BOARD THE DISTANCE FROM
TOP OF PLATFORM TO WATER LEVEL WOULD BE 1-3"

The new vessel was Lloyd's registered and accurate detail of its dimensions, classification and engines are recorded. It is shown as having been of iron and steel construction, built by Alley and Maclennan Ltd of Glasgow in January 1915. It measured 56ft long, 18ft broad but its depth is not given. It had a total length over the gangways of 74ft. The 12hp engine had 2 cylinders of 6 and 6½in. The boiler of the Cochrane type made by Campbell and Calderwood of Paisley, worked at a pressure of 90lbs. It needed 5cwts (500 kg) of coal daily. The hull was divided into five watertight compartments by cross bulkheads. It could carry four cars at one crossing.

38693 Windermere Ferry Iron&Steel
ssBonessNo.3–5,24
ssBonessNo.1–28
1Dk(Stl)

✠ A–
4,30
BS4,30 ✠LMC5,28
For Ferry purposes on Lake Winde

Bo-
ness

19
1

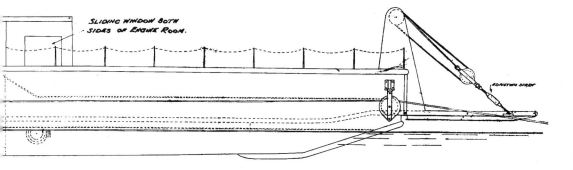

Plans of the 1915 Ferry are lodged in the County Record Office in Kendal. They show details of the landing ramp adjustment mechanism, which allowed the ferrymen to alter the ramp angle from their control position.

Leslie Hewkin in Cumbria Magazine (May 1954) calculated that in its forty years of service the 1915 Ferry made more than a million crossings and sailed some 350,000 miles. It was replaced in 1954, and was sold to Carruthers of Dumfries as scrap for £53. It is believed the boiler was removed to Kentmere Limited for use as a steam generator. The whereabouts of the brass plaque, visible on some photographs, is unknown.

&	CountyCouncilsof	56·0|18·0|			2Cy.6'-6½"	
lan,Ld	Westmorland&			British	100℔	3NℍP
•w	Lancashire(Wind-		FK	4BHAsp	1B,ɢs6,ʜs80	
	ermereFerryJoint				Campbell&Calderw'd,Psy.	
	Sub-Committee,					
	Mgrs.)					

Excerpt from Lloyds Register of Ships.

Coaling-up (Fuelling) 1930s era, Ferry Nab.
Late Kenneth Shepherd

1954 THE 'DRAKE'

58664	DRAKE		70	COUNTY COUNCILS OF	British	✠A
			—	WESTMORLAND &		for ferry service on
			50	LANCASHIRE		Lake Windermere
				Windermere Ferry Joint		✠LMC
				Sub-Committee		
	S Chain Ferry		7–1954	S 2Cy. 6″ × 7″		
	Lytham S.B. & E. Co. Ltd.		Lytham	LythamS.B.&Co.Ltd.		Lytham
	95′ 0″ 30′ 0″ 1′ 10″	1 dk ptEW		1 VB 110℔		ND

Excerpt from Lloyd's Register of Ships.

The 1954 Ferry was the first to have a name. The 'Drake' was so called after a well-known Lancashire County Surveyor. The Lytham Shipbuilding and Engineering Company Limited built the new boat. She was of 70 tons gross registered weight, and was 95ft in overall length and 30ft broad. Assembly from prefabricated parts took place on the Lakeside slip. She was powered by a 2 cylinder steam engine with a boiler pressure of 110lbs, which needed 1 ton (2000kg) of coal daily. The same company that built the boat built the engine. It could carry ten cars and the total cost was £29,825.

758. Windermere Ferry Boat "Drake".

'Drake' making across a rough Lake in the 1950s.

The new ferry went into service on 13th July 1954. On its first trip it carried a number of trucks filled with sand weighing about ninety tons to check its stability. A number of post-commissioning faults had to be rectified. The decking of narrow slats proved capable of trapping the heels of ladies' shoes and was uneven, new timber treads were laid. The open cabin doors were a problem in inclement weather and sliding doors were fitted. The fuel used made thick black smoke, which gave rise to complaints, including smoke staining of clothing. It proved impossible to obtain Welsh smokeless fuel and trials of smokeless gas coke were made, which proved effective. There was rapid wear on the cast-iron driving wheel rims, and these were replaced with cast steel.

By 1960 the steam engine was considered to be inefficient and it was replaced by two Leyland diesel engines of 320 horse power with hydrostatic transmission, costing £7,750. The engines burnt one gallon of diesel fuel per hour. The fuel tank held five hundred gallons and was refilled every five weeks. The conversion was projected to reduce the annual fuel cost from £2500 for coal to £300 for diesel oil. The boat's maximum speed was eight knots, but its usual cruising speed was five knots. In 1966 annual takings for the year were £12,000. The boat continued in use until 1990 when it was scrapped.

Leyland plan showing the arrangement of diesel machinery and final drive unit.
Reproduced with permission from the British Commercial Vehicle Museum Trust

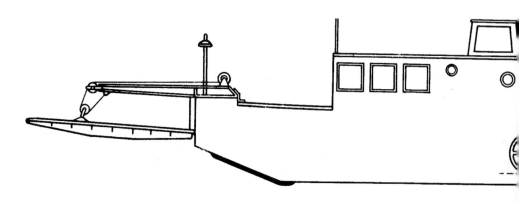

Testing the diesel conversion's ability to hold the Ferry on the landing when a heavy lorry disembarks.

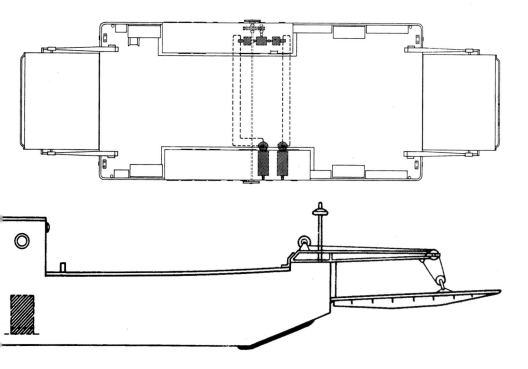

The Ferry, Lake Windermere. s.320.

Sanderson and Dixon post card showing the 'Drake' fully loaded – before diesel conversion.

The 'Drake' approaching Ferry Nab in November 1989. It's splendid chimney had been removed after conversion to diesel.

The Drake at Lakeside in March 1990 – waiting sadly for the breakers.

1990 THE 'MALLARD'

The name for the new boat was chosen from more than one hundred and twenty suggestions made by the public. An article in The Lakeland Echo of 3rd May 1990 gives the following description of the new ferry. Cumbria County Council's design brief for a new ferry was for a design, construct, deliver, launch and commission contract. The new ferry was required to carry one hundred passengers and eighteen average sized cars, or a combination of cars, trucks and coaches together with one hundred passengers. It was to be a single deck, double ended, roll on/roll off, cable-driven ferry with landing ramps at each end discharging onto the existing slipways. FL Steelcraft of Borth, in Wales was the successful company.

The 'Mallard' is largely constructed from Lloyd's Register of Shipping grade steel. However, appreciable quantities of timber, glass, rubber and aluminium have also been used. The superstructure, interiors and exteriors of the vessel are all painted with corrosion-resistant epoxy paint. The car deck, passenger walkways and the accommodation floors are covered with anti-slip paint. The quick release deck hatches are manufactured from aluminium and provide easy access below deck. The passenger accommodation seating, all doors, cabinets, lockers and the control console in the wheelhouse are of hardwood timber. Some of

A view of the 'Mallard' on the slip at Calgarth.

Commissioning the 'Mallard' at Ferry Nab in April 1990.

Ferryman Arthur Wilson standing by the engine of the Mallard on 29th January 2002.

the statistics for materials used include: steel - 100 tonnes; glass - 21 square metres; hardwood timber - 20 square metres; paint - 1,500 litres; anti-slip paint - 540 litres. There is heated passenger accommodation for 30, and covered accommodation for a further 40. Foot passengers can join and leave the boat without using the vehicle access ways. The total cost was £480,000.

The design architect of the boat was Mr Dennis Swire of Portleven, Cornwall. Mr E.F. Bentley who was ferry manager at that time, assisted by Mr J. Dickenson of Hull, a consultant naval architect, supervised the assembly of the boat.

The boat was constructed on the White Cross slip at Calgarth, from prefabricated units made in Wales and transported to the site by road. The launch proved difficult, as the concrete apron, a relic of Short's wartime Sunderland Flying Boat factory, collapsed and had to be covered with 300 iron sheets.

After 1990 the Ferry was no longer classified as a vessel and therefore does not appear in subsequent registers of shipping.

'Mallard' started operation in April 1990. She suffered a number of faults in her early years. In April 1992 she needed major repairs, and was out of use for a number of days while the drive shaft was replaced. In May 1992 a collision occurred which showed that even the large size of the new boat did not discourage the foolhardy from venturing too close. As a sign of the times the offending boat this time was a jet ski. In 1994 an analysis of stoppages showed that high winds were causing increased lost operating hours. In 1993 some 3% of operating hours were lost for mechanical or weather reasons.

'Mallard' mid-lake on 22 January 2002.

Table 2 to
Agenda Item No 7
WFASC 02/02/95

WINDERMERE FERRY LOG SUMMARY
SUSPENSION OF SERVICE RECORDS 1994

Report No	Day	Date	Off	On	Hours	Reason
130	Wed	12/01/94	09.30	14.30	5.00	High Winds
131	Thurs	13/01/94	13.30	21.10	7.66	High Winds
132	Tues	18/01/94	16.30	21.10	4.66	High Winds
133	Wed	26/01/94	17.30	18.50	1.33	High Winds
134	Tues	08/03/94	14.45	18.00	3.25	High Winds
135	Sun	13/03/94	09.30	21.10	11.66	High Winds
136	Mon	14/03/94	12.00	13.30	1.50	High Winds
137	Wed	23/03/94	09.50	14.50	5.00	High Winds
138	Wed	20/03/94	19.30	21.10	1.66	High Winds
139	Tues	31/03/94	06.50	21.10	14.33	High Winds
140	Mon	11/04/94	06.50	-	629.86**)	4 Yearly Major Overhaul
	Sun	22/05/94	-	22.10	)	
141	Sat	28/05/94	11.00	15.00	4.00	Floating Pulley Seized
142	Tues	31/05/94	19.30	22.10	2.66	Modify Floating Pulley
143	Sun	05/06/94	16.30	18.30	2.00	Fuel Blockage
144	Thurs	15/09/94	21.00	22.10	1.16	High Winds
145	Fri	04/11/94	09.00	16.45	7.75*	Cable Change
146	Sun	13/11/94	17.45	21.10	3.41	Strong Wind/High Water
147	Mon	14/11/94	06.50	21.10	14.33	High Water
148	Thurs	08/12/94	06.50	09.10	2.33	Very Strong Winds
149	Sat	10/12/94	12.50	21.10	8.33	Very Strong Winds
150	Sun	11/12/94	09.50	21.10	11.33	Very Strong Winds
151	Wed	28/12/94	08.00	21.10	13.16	Very Strong Winds
152	Thurs	29/12/94	06.50	08.00	1.17	Very Strong Winds

*   Planned stoppage - cable replacement
**   Planned stoppage - major overhaul, passenger launch provided

Copy of Windermere Ferry Log Summary Suspension of Service Records 1994.
Cumbria County Council Minutes 1995

Table 1 to
Agenda Item No 7
WFASC 02/02/95

MAJOR OVERHAUL COSTS

1	Planned Work	Original Estimate (£)	Actual Cost (£)
	Towage, Slipping, Slipway Hire*	25 000	61 032.60
	Engines Overhaul	10 000	11 349.01
	Hydraulics	8 000	15 208.70
	Paintwork	8 000	22 633.67
	Welding	5 000	11 000
	Drive Wheel Improvement	7 000	6 625.20
	Pedestrian Launch	11 000	13 256.04
	Miscellaneous items, supervision, specialist consultants	10 000	16 425.00
	Contingencies	6 000	-
		90 000	157 524.17

2	Unplanned Work		
	Bilge System Improvement		5 235.97
	Electrical System Improvement		2 758.73
	Extra Cranage		2 808.95
	Diving Inspections		453.60
	Lap Board Repairs		8 733.00
	Mechanical Checking of Shaft and Seals		3 527.11
	Barrier Repairs		1 174.15
	Mooring Bollards Provision		864.00
	Hull Joint Strengthening		10 585.07
	Additional Supervision/Coordination		17 390.95
			53 531.53

3	Total		211 055.70

*Includes slipway widening and steelwork

Major Overhaul Costs – 1994.   *Cumbria County Council Minutes 1995*

Chapter Three

THE GREAT FERRY
ACCIDENT OF 1635

A number of sources make reference to the accident in 1635 in which almost fifty people drowned. It is believed that late on the 19th October 1635, the ferry boat became loaded with a large party returning from a wedding and the market in Hawkshead. The large number involved and the presence of accompanying horses and possibly carriages indicates the boat was at, or near, capacity. Stormy weather is known to have been occurring at the time as it is recorded that the River Kent came into the vestry of Kendal Parish Church. Explanations of the cause of the accident are not available, but it may be assumed that overloading and rough conditions caused the boat to founder and the passengers put into the water. None survived.

The dead are listed in the Grasmere Parish Register, which is in itself a curiosity; since other sources record that the dead were buried in the grounds of St Martin's Church in Bowness. The entry in the Grasmere Register was made in 1641. Miss Armitt, in her History of the Church of Grasmere suggests George Bennison who was clerk and schoolmaster in Grasmere made the entry. She thought he might have had the intention of recording local history. The Windermere Parish Register for the period 1628 to 1643 is missing.

The list of the dead is as follows:

> Mr George Wilson of Kendall
> John Beck, his wife, his son, and a servant maide of Kendall
> Thomas Powe of Kendall
> Randall Noble of Kendall
> John Kitchens son of Strickland feild
> John Pearson and his wife of Skelsmore
> Christofer Phillipson of Ashes

Gervis Stricklands wife of Staveley

Mary daughter of John Phillipson

Thomas Milner boateman and his two daughters

Henry Pearson and Dorothie his sister

Tho: Bateman of Crooke

James Warriner of the same

John Satterwayte of the same

Christopher Willans wife

Rolland Strickland

Myles Powe

Anthony Sewart

Anthony Elleray

Richard Robinson

Thomas Parke son of Rolland

Willm Park of Colgarth

James Sewart

Myles Birkehead - son of Myles

Willm Roberts son of Thomas

Christoph: Parke of Colgarth Willms brother

Willm Rawes

Thomas Woods wife

Nicholas Bell wife

George Baxter and his wife

John Rowanson

Willm Holme

Richard Robinson

Willm Sewarts wife

Richard Scills daughter

Mark Harrinsons wife

Arthur Ellis

Myles Rigge

and 2 more or 3 and 7 horses and one that escaped.

Of those named thirty-one were male and fourteen female. Among them were family groups and relatives. Adding up the list of names a total of forty-eight passengers can be deduced, though the last line leaves the possibility there were forty-nine. In addition 'seven horses and one that escaped' can be taken to mean that seven horses drowned and one horse escaped. The traditional burial site in Bowness Church Yard is known as the 'eight and forty row,' which tends to confirm the forty-

Windermere Ferry Pre 1870 steam days – similarities may be drawn here to the 1635 disaster! Taken from a faded print. *Late Eric Clark*

eight total. The burial site was cut into in 1871 when the chancel of the church was extended, and there is now nothing to indicate where it was.

Confirmation of the identity of some of the group can be gained by examining the contemporary parish registers and the accounts of the accident that have survived. From the Hawkshead Parish Register it can be established that no weddings took place on 19th October 1635, but two occurred on the 18th. These were of Richard Wilson and Agnes Scales, and William Sawrey and Thomasin Strickland. Evidence from a book published in 1636 and called 'The Fatall Nuptial,' thought to be by Richard Brathwaite of Burneside Hall, suggests that it was the latter pair whose wedding guests were affected. Brathwaite wrote in his preamble 'Amongst which, the Bride's Mother and her Brother in this liquid regiment, equally perished.' The list of the dead contains the names of Gervis Strickland's wife of Staveley and Rolland Strickland. The Kendal (Holy Trinity) Parish Register shows that Jarvis Strickland of Staveley had a daughter Thomazin, baptised on 11th October 1612. There is nothing to suggest that the bride and bridegroom were drowned. Indeed the Hawkshead Parish Register records the burial of a still born child to William Sawrey on July 12th 1636 and his wife Thomasin, was buried in the church on July 25th 1636. William remarried in 1638.

There are some facts known about others who drowned. W.G. Collingwood in an article about 'The Fatall Nuptial' mentions George

Wilson, who appears to have been an attorney in the common law. Kendal records show that a George Wilson was elected one of twenty-four assistants on 18th April 1633 and Chamberlain in 1634, but that he died and was replaced in 1635. Miss Armitt in her notes for her History of the Church of Grasmere records that the registers of Windermere Church show the existence of Thomas Milner, boatman, who is included in the list of the drowned with his two daughters, Elizabeth and Alice, who would have been nineteen and sixteen at the time of the accident.

There are two accounts of the accident in local literature. One, already referred to, is 'The Fatall Nuptial' which is attributed to Richard Brathwaite of Burneside Hall, an established author who published numerous tracts between 1611 and 1665. The book is extremely rare and a single copy is kept in the Bodleian Library in Oxford. W.G. Collingwood (Ruskin's secretary) published an article about this poem in the 1920s. A letter in the Manchester City News from a Mr K. Hughes of Kersal drew his attention to it in 1912. Mr Hughes had prepared a transcript presumably from the original Latin, which he had presented to the Cumberland and Westmorland Antiquarian and Archaeological Society. As mentioned earlier the preamble contains significant clues to the identity of the drowned, and is also seen to be one of the first accounts to recognise the picturesque qualities of the Lake District.

Preamble

For the quality of griefe, none knows it, but hee who hath experimentally and personally felt it. That Place, which hath hitherto beene secured from the least perill, you shall now see personated a spectacle of sorrow: where those, who vowed in a Sacred and Christian manner, their vowes to Hymen, the Soveraigne of Nuptialls, are now with Tethis to close in wat'ry Funeralls. The occasion of these sad Obits proceeded from a marriage and a market day, which begot to the Attendants a mournefull night: yet from that night (such was their assured expectance, and our undoubted affiance) a happy day. The place, where these drenched Soules were to take Boate, was that famous and renowned mere of Windermere; a Mere no less eminent and generously known for her Sole-breeding, and peculiar kinde of fishes (commonly called Chares) as for those windy and labyrinthian mazes, with those curiously shaded, beauteously tufted, naturally fortifide, and impregnably seated Ilands in every part of the mere interveined. To relate the severall windings of it, or more historically to describe it, were fruitles, being already explained by a genuine and learned relater. To divert them from this Place, to the sad occasion of this Action, thus I proceed.

Windermere, or Winandermere, streaming, or rather staying in a continuate Tract or Channell, without any visible or apparent Current, and dividing the Counties of Westmerland and Lancashire, hath ever constantly kept a Boat for Passengers; especially those Inhabitants as remaine or reside in the Barrorny of Kendall, (a place to her honour, antiently famous for Commerce and industrious Manufacture) as all others, who may have occasion to addresse their course by that passage, to the market of Haukeside, or other places adjoining. To this Boat, upon a nuptiall but fatall occasion, sundry passengers, and these all Inhabitants within the Barrorny of Kendall, (a Burrough as I formerly observed, highly eminent, by having such neare relation and general correspondence with most places of trade or trafficke in this Kingdome) repaired; hoping with a safe and secure gale to arrive, where no perill had ever yet approach'd. The Boat they enter'd, securely confident, with 47 in number, besides other carriages and horses, which (together with the roughness of the water, and extremity of weather) occasioned this inevitable danger.

Lanch'd had these scarcely to the medth of the water, being scantly a mile broad, but the boat, either through the pressure and weight which surcharg'd her, or some violent and impetuous windes and waves that surpriz'd her, with all her people, became drenchd in the depths. No succour, no reliefe afforded, for God's definite Will had so decreed: So as, not one person of all the number was saved: Amongst which, the Bride's Mother, and her Brother in this liquid regiment, equally perished.

The poem itself, a moralising tale, embellished with imagined details of the catastrophe, gives few further clues either to the cause of the accident or the character of the drowned.

Mr Hughes' letter in the Manchester City News contains an amusing misunderstanding of the reference in the preamble to 'Sole-breeding and peculiar kinde of fishes' (commonly called Chares). Mr Hughes commented, 'I cannot explain the reference to 'Sole-breeding' on Lake Windermere. It is true that soles sometimes make their way up the estuaries and some distance up rivers, but the best authorities are agreed that soles never under any circumstances breed in fresh water. Nor can I find any dialect in England in which 'sole' is used to denote any other species of fish.' Clearly Mr Hughes did not grasp that 'Sole-breeding' referred to the char which Brathwaite thought only occurred in Windermere (it is of course known now that char occur in many other lakes).

Cowper in his 'History of Hawkshead' records that the accident was also captured in verse by Auld Hoggart of Troutbeck (Thomas Hoggart). He wrote:

'Upon the 19th Day of October 1635 the great boat upon Windermere water sunck about sun setting, when was drowned fforty seavan persons and eleavan horses: form suden Death Libera nos.'

Followed by an Epitaph:

Weepe not sweet friends, but wipe away all teares,
We are delivered from all human feares;
Let no man rashly judge of this our fall,
But rather let's a warning be to all,
And let none censure what we did,
Our thoughts were known to God, to mortals hid;
And though our bodye's sinke into the deape,
Our souls did mount, and therefore do not weepe.

Some curious correspondence in the Westmorland Gazette in 1915 adds a mysterious dimension to the puzzle over why the deaths are recorded in the Grasmere Parish Register. The letters were stimulated by the replacement of the first steam ferry by a new boat. On 16th January a letter signed E. I. commented on the history of the service and recalled the 1635 accident, noting that the Grasmere Parish Register was the only source from which the names of those who perished could be gleaned. On 23rd January a reply from W.F. Rawnsley of Sharnley Green, Guildford was published. It said, "if your correspondent E. I. who writes about the Windermere Ferry disaster in 1635 will turn to Miss Armitt's book 'The Church of Grasmere' he (or she) will see that the names of the drowned are not to be found in the Grasmere Register, and will also learn why they are not to be found elsewhere." On 30th January another letter on the subject, this time from H.F. Wilson, points out that Miss Armitt's book does indeed contain a description of the entry in the register giving the names of the dead. He further points out that H.S. Cowper in his History of Hawkshead also confirms there is an entry. Mr Wilson then comments that since Mr Rawnsley prepared Miss Armitt's book for the press (he was her literary mentor), "he should know all there is to know about the affair." He concludes that Mr Rawnsley's letter is, "somewhat mystifying." A study of Mr Rawnsley's letters to Miss Armitt, preserved in the Armitt library, throws no light on the mystery.

In the annals of ferry accidents, the 1635 disaster at Windermere is high on the list. However it is by no means the worst.

BRITISH FERRY ACCIDENTS

YEAR	PLACE	NO. DROWNED
1809	MEIKLE (DORNAY FIRTH)	99
1785	MENAI (CAERNARVON - ABERMENAI)	54
1529	CAMBUSKENNETH (FIRTH OF FORTH)	50
1635	WINDERMERE	48
1589	BURNTISLAND (FIRTH OF FORTH)	41
1553	GRAVESEND (R. THAMES)	30 OR 40
1723	MENAI	30
1876	ABERDEEN (R.DEE)	30
1616	SOUTHWOLD - WALBERSWICK (R.BLYTH)	22
1796	KING'S LYNN (WASH)	22
1815	NEWPORT (R.TAY)	22

This information was taken from – 'Ferries and Ferrymen' by G.Bernard Wood, and 'Ferries in Scotland' by Marie Weir.

Most accidents were caused by overcrowding and inclement weather. Despite legislation passed at various times limiting numbers of passengers per boat, accidents continued. The lure of extra revenue defeating the good intentions of the legislators.

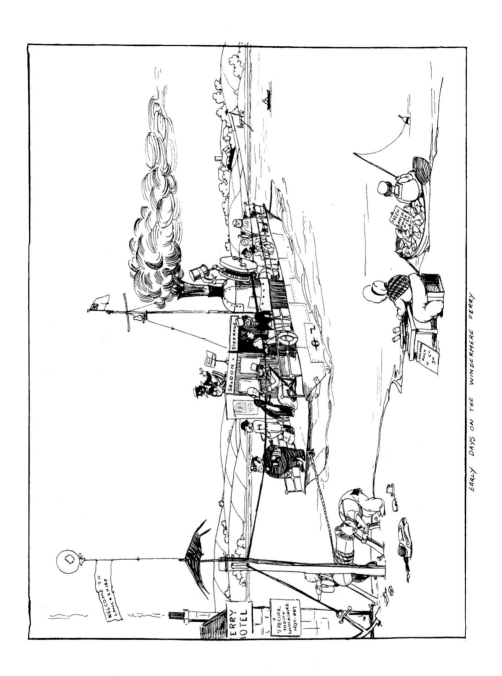

A present given to the late Eric Clark.

Chapter Four

FERRY OWNERS

As discussed in Chapter One, the early origins of the Windermere Ferry are unclear, however Charlotte Kipling, in her survey of the commercial fisheries of Windermere, cites a 1454 rental of the Earl of Richmond which states, 'that the men who paid rent for two parts of the Windermere fishery refused to pay for the ferrying rights because Henry Bellyngham 'farmer of the fishery' claimed these rights.' Henry is the first named ferry operator to be so identified. Whether he operated a ferry on the line of the present service is open to question. Cowper, in his book on Hawkshead, cites a number of documents containing references to ferries and ferriage, but he shows they apply to carriage of goods in all parts of the lake as well as the 'ferry proper.'

Cowper lists later documents identifying other ferry operators. In 1575 a dispute between ferriers resulted in an award giving Myles Milner the right to ferry in the middle cubble both for horse and man, or any other carriage that shall be requested of him. Windermere was divided into three cubbles for fishery purposes. The origin of the word 'cubble' is obscure. The English Dialect Dictionary gives several meanings, which include a short, flat-bottomed rowing boat as well as a large sea-going sailing fishing vessel. The word 'coble' is used in Northumberland to describe the right for salmon fishing with a coble (rowing boat) or an area of water. This is a likely source of the word cubble used on Windermere to define an area of fishing.

A document of 1670 made an award to Thomas Braithwaite who 'had due and right to ferry and carry over all and every the said cubles both horse and man and all sorts of goods and commodities whatsoever to his best advantage.' In 1699 an agreement was made involving Miles Sandys and William Rawlinson, both of Graythwaite, and Oliver Sandys of Sawrey and a number of other residents to fund an action against Thomas Braithwaite who intended to increase the ferry fare. In 1707 Thomas Braithwaite conveyed two ferry boats, the ferry passage and a parcel of land to William Rawlinson of Graythwaite. Later the same year Rawlinson transferred the rights to William Braithwaite of Satterhow. The agreement contained a clause that the boats should not ever be sold to anyone on the Westmorland side. W.T. McIntire, in a posthumous article in the Cumberland News (25th November 1944) notes that in 1711 George Braithwaite complains that, 'whereas he and those whose estate he had, from time immemorable lawfully possessed a common ferry boat upon Windermere Water ... nevertheless Thomas Elleray, of Storrs, John Elleray of the same, and George Robinson of Undermillock, yeomen, forcibly kept a ferry boat upon the said water.' The Braithwaites seem afterwards to have been concerned in a fight in which one of the oars of the boat was thrown into the water and lost. George Braithwaite and a friend were indicted for assault, and Braithwaite was fined 2s 6d.

The Ferry Rights have often been in dispute, an example can be seen in this document from the Graythwaite Papers in Lancashire Record Office.

The written opinion of William Rawlinson re powers of George Braithwaite to ferry on Windermere – mid 18th century (DDSA 27/3 not dated). Reproduced with the permission of Mr M. Sandys of Graythwaite.   *Lancashire Record Office*

The right of renting the ferry passed with the purchase of Ambleside Hall to Thomas Dummer, and from him to Sir William Fleming. This Fleming connection is confirmed by a letter dated 13th September 1726 in the Rydal Hall papers. Sir William wrote to Thomas Dummer complaining that the right of the owner of Ambleside Hall to keep boats on Windermere was in danger of being lost through non-usage. His complaint was against the man who had purchased the 'Ferry passage cross Windermere Water near the middle of it,' and was, 'labouring to impress himself the sole privaledge of carrying goods upon the said water to advance the price of it as much as he pleased.' He was concerned that the 'Stuard of the Lonsdale Court' had been hastily inveigled into impaling a jury to consider the problem, but Sir William had managed to get the hearing adjourned. The letter suggested that Mr Dummer might influence some of his tenants in the matter. This dispute must have been provoked by a 1726 document, which shows that George Braithwaite of the Boat was claiming sole ferriage up and down the lake.

Bruce Thompson, in his essay, next records the ownership as passing to Thomas English who commenced building his famous 'pepper pot' house on Belle Isle in 1764. English sold his estate to the Trustees of the young Isabella Curwen, heiress of Workington Hall in 1781. In 1800 a document names John Christian Curwen claiming he has an exclusive right to ferriage. During the Curwen's ownership of the ferry it was leased to other individuals who were tenants of the Ferry Inn. In 1831 Thomas Cloudsdale (later licensee of the Crown Inn in Bowness) took a seven year lease at a rent of £75. The lease contained conditions, one of which being that he should at all times keep in good order and repair the boats for conveying passengers over Windermere Water and once in every year paint pitch coak[1] and put in repair the Little Boat, and the Great Boat every two years.

Between 1879 and 1881 a new Ferry Hotel was built and the first tenant, W.B. Logan, took not only the hotel but also the ferrying rights. This was later to change when the local authority wished to take it over and bring it into public ownership.

The 1913 minutes of the Westmorland County Council show that they were interested in taking over the operation of the Windermere Ferry. At their meeting of 5th September 1913 a letter from Windermere Urban District Council was considered. The letter suggested that it would be desirable that a better and more efficient service between Windermere and Hawkshead be established and that the hours of service be extended. The matter was referred to the Main Roads Committee for consideration and report. This committee, at its meeting on 11th October 1913 resolved that a prima facie case had been made for the appointment of a Sub-Committee to obtain information with a view to establish a better and more efficient Ferry Service across the lake between Ferry Nab on the Westmorland side and the Ferry on the Lancashire side, and to consult with other bodies if desirable. Sub-Committee to consist of Aichison Browne, G.H. Pattinson (Convener), Cropper, Weston, Greenall, Hamilton and Ward-Shane. An appendix to

1 Coak - caulking to seal the gaps in the planking.

A cart and horse being conveyed on a still morning on the Horse Ferry and the Old Ferry Inn in the background.
Late Charlotte Kipling

the minutes of 20th February 1914 included a resolution that the lessee of the ferry be approached to see if he would be prepared to negotiate respecting an improved service for the same. On 15th March 1914 a letter from Messrs Gatey Son and Healey, Solicitors of Ambleside pointed out, '… that Mr Logan is this year renewing his lease of the ferry and has at the present time in course of construction a new Ferry Boat built under Lloyd's inspection which is larger and more commodious than the existing one and one that he feels confident will meet all the requirements and convenience of the public.' It was resolved that the matter be not proceeded with at present, the Council to await results of the works contemplated by Mr Logan for the improvement of the service.

It was not until 1920 that the Council felt able to return to the matter. On 7th February 1920 the minutes of Westmorland County Council record that it was resolved that the Council is favourable to the acquisition in conjunction with Lancashire County Council of the rights of ferrying across Windermere. Arrangements to be made for transfer of the ferry to a public authority. The operation of the Ferry became the responsibility of the Lancashire and Westmorland Joint Ferry Sub-Committee in 1920.

On 27th February 1920 it was resolved that the ferry be taken over from the present lessees by the Joint Councils in equal share as from 1st March 1920. The boats and equipment being purchased for £3665-4s-0d, half being paid by Lancashire and half by Westmorland.

It was further resolved that the County Surveyor be asked to undertake the management of the ferry. Some form of ticket or check for passengers should be instituted, but that the County Surveyor of Westmorland be requested to draw up a scheme for the better management of the Ferry and the taking of the tolls, and submit it to the Joint Committee at an early date. In the meantime the County Surveyor be authorised to arrange with the ferrymen an increase of wages, which was immediately overdue.

Following local government reorganisation in 1974, the ownership of the Windermere Ferry passed to Cumbria County Council. The Lancashire and Westmorland Joint Ferry Committee was replaced by the Windermere Ferry Advisory Committee. The new committee met once annually, usually in Windermere. Its predecessor had met at least twice yearly, or more frequently if it had business to consider. The new Committee's terms of reference were to consult with representatives of South Lakeland District Council, the Claife and Windermere Parish

Councils, and such other local interests as were appropriate on specific matters affecting the ferry service, and to make recommendations to the County Council's Highways and Transportation Committee. The composition of the first committee, which met on 11th October 1974 was: Cumbria County Council - Mr E.J. Barker, Mr J. Bibby, Mr W.D. Cooper, Revd. J.P. Inman and Mr G.E. Mason; South Lakeland District Council - Mr E.R. Capstick, Mrs C. Thornton; Lake District Special Planning Board - Mrs M. Capstick, and Mrs I. James; Windermere Parish Council - Mr J. Davidson and Mr L. Fitzjames; and Claife Parish Council - Mr T.P. Naylor.

The business of the Committee soon settled into a regular pattern involving financial, operational and miscellaneous items. Perhaps because it met less frequently and was composed of fewer local people, the Committee's business seems to have lost its 'hands on' style and laid more emphasis on future planning and finance. The change was gradual and in the late 70s and early 80s discussions about operational detail and facilities still frequently featured on the agenda. Another change gradually became apparent in that it was possible to discern, in the minutes, an increasing polarisation between the representative groups and the County Council members. These strains must have come to a head, when in 1984 it was discovered that constitutionally only the County Council members could vote. The representative groups had no vote! It was not until 1987 that it was conceded the representative groups could have one vote per authority. However, this still left the County Council in numerical superiority.

Those who attended Committee Meetings could detect an increasing almost 'class warfare' element to the discussions. It appeared to some that the representatives of the industrial parts of West Cumberland and Barrow resented the 'country landowners' influence from Claife. The inference being that in the past the privileged class had rigged the Ferry's fare structure to benefit local people at the expense of tourists and others.

Frequent items under discussion were the price of annual contracts, priority crossing for local residents and the 'Reserve Fund'. The Reserve Fund had always been a feature of ferry budgeting. It was intended to provide adequate finance for the major overhauls and to provide for a replacement boat when that became necessary. By 1990 when 'Drake' was replaced by 'Mallard' at a cost of almost half a million pounds, the Reserve Fund did indeed cover the outlay. However, through the 1990s the fund began to fall behind. At the Advisory Committee meeting in

54

February 1995 Windermere Parish Council expressed concern that local views proposed and accepted by the Advisory Committee were constantly not being taken into consideration by the County Council, and that financial surpluses created by the Ferry were not being retained solely for the benefit of ferry users and the ferry itself.

The new ferry 'Mallard', with its greater carrying capacity had turned into a significant revenue earner. The County Council had begun to cream off surplus funds for use elsewhere in its budget and by 1995 the ferry service had contributed £150,000 to the Council's coffers. At the Committee's meeting in February 1999, the non-County Council members and County Councillor Mrs Parker expressed concern that the Reserve Fund was not accumulating as projected and that if the present trend of just building up sufficient to cover the five yearly overhauls continued, there would be insufficient money available for replacement of the Ferry at the end of its thirty year life. The County Council members pointed out that the ferry was owned by the Council and it was the Council's responsibility, which included its replacement.

This assurance did not allay the local representatives' anxieties, and at the December 1999 Meeting the County Council had to spell out its position again by minuting, 'County Council members appreciated the concerns expressed, but pointed out the Ferry was owned by the County Council and that the onus lay with the Council to replace it, regardless of whether the reserve fund could stand the cost.' Thus the future replacement of the Windermere Ferry seems secure.

W.B. Logan – Tenant of Ferry Hotel.
Master of Coniston Foxhounds and
Windermere Harriers.
Bruce Logan (great nephew)

W.B. Logan with his grandson B.L.
Thompson (author of Anitquarian
Essay on Windermere Ferry) –
behind the Ferry Hotel.
Bruce Logan

Chapter Five

FERRYMEN

To passengers the visible face of the ferry was the crew. There must have been many individuals who fulfilled this role. Each would have had a personality, which would have been remembered for some quality. Sadly relatively few have been captured in recorded history. George Robinson, a ferryman known to William Wordsworth is one exception, and an account of him is given in T.W. Thompson's 'Wordsworth's Hawkshead.' Cowper records the name of John Long as being well-remembered as chief boatman at the Ferry in about 1811. He died in 1848. Cowper quotes A. Craig Gibson's poem about the Calgarth Skulls.

'And Benjamin's chief ferryman was stalwart old John Long'

Census records from 1841 show numerous residents of Sawrey as having boatman as their occupation, but this may not necessarily relate to the Ferry. The 1871 census shows Geoffrey Dickson aged twenty-six and Braithwaite Barker aged sixty-two, residing at the Ferry Hotel and having as occupation Boatman - Ferry.

Bruce Thompson records that when W.B. Logan took the new Ferry Hotel in 1880, he employed two ferrymen, William Mortlock and Thomas Clement. The financial arrangements seemed curious. Mr Logan kept the Windermere Harriers on the proceeds of operating the ferry. It seemed common knowledge that he expected £1000 per annum from the ferry operation for that purpose. The rest was kept by the crew. An account in the North Lonsdale Magazine in 1899, names Isaac Brockbank as the ferryman. Bulmer's Directory (1911) shows James Coward, of Town End, as a ferryman, and Joseph Prickett Strickland, of Fair Rigg, as ferry boat skipper.

John Edward Atkinson commenced work as a ferryman in 1910. He was born near Coniston and was brought up in Sawrey, attending Hawkshead Grammar School. His first job was working for his uncle

Possibly Jim Coward pre 1915.   *Late Eric Clark*

who was a partner in a Liverpool Estate Agents. For six years John collected rents from slum properties. The business declined when his uncle died. He returned to the Lake District and worked for Sir Edward Holt of Blackwell, driving a steam launch, and also Ben Townson's (of Storrs) electric launches. In about 1910 when he was working as a forester at Graythwaite, Mr Logan, knowing of his experience with launches, asked him to become ferryman. The wage was £1.1s.0d (£1.05) per week, plus three meals a day in the hotel, but his wage was supplemented by tips. He had to be up at 4.15 am and on the boat by 5.15 am in order to have enough steam to run the first trip at 7 am. There was no shelter from the weather on the old boat and often he would have been 'drier in t'lake.' In his 28 years of service he carried many strange cargoes and eminent people, including Lord Simon (a former Foreign Secretary and Chancellor of the Exchequer) and Professor Joad. On his retirement in 1938 he was presented with a grandmother clock bearing the inscription 'Presented to John Atkinson by his friends of the parish of Sawrey, as a mark of

Johnnie Atkinson with his wife, who lived to the right old age of 105!   *Late Eric Clark*

Johnnie Atkinson – taken in 1930s aboard the ferry by Atkinson and
Pollitt of Kendal. *Late Eric Clark*

appreciation on his retirement, after 28 years service on the
Windermere ferry boat.' His wife survived to the age of 105.

Talking to Leslie Hewkin in Cumbria Magazine May, 1954 he
recalled some unusual experiences. 'In those days 'cow jobbers' [1] used to
travel round the farms buying an odd cow here and there which were
then driven to an auction in Kendal. A Joe Abbot, of Crosthwaite, was
such a jobber and on one occasion he crossed the lake with his cattle
without incident. When they landed on the Windermere side the cattle
split, some going up the road and the others onto the Nab. These sur-
veyed the lake, waded into the water and then decided to go back to
Sawrey. By this time Joe had made off up the road with the others, leaving John alone. Fortunately a boatman, George Walker, was in a nearby
punt, which he manoeuvred to the low side of the ferryboat. The two

1 Cow Jobber - A dealer in cows

9th October 1933 Johnnie Atkinson and Henry Leigh Groves passing the time of day with fish van already on board with wicker basket on roof. *Late Eric Clark*

made their way slowly across to the Ferry Hotel side, keeping the cattle bunched together between the two boats. "We managed to get them across with only two breakaways," related John. "When we landed, all the hotel visitors were on the lawn to greet us. The licensee, Mr Logan, was at home and he took charge of the seven or eight beasts, fastening them up in his stables." John then returned to normal service. On arrival at the other side he found Joe busy scanning the lake. "Hev they gone to t'bottom?" he shouted, "I can't see 'em." A look of relief came on his face when he heard the story. He had given the cattle up as soon as they got out off their depth, deciding to cut his losses and chase the others to the Rectory Farm, where he tied them up. "You know, I got nowt for my trouble and George didn't either," commented John.

On another occasion it was a local man who took a plunge. John bid him good night and immediately afterwards heard a splash in the dark. The man had walked off the wrong end. "What a job I had lifting him on board again. I took him shivering to the Hotel bar, where he was soon rigged up in dry clothes." He also told of another man doing record time down Ferry Hill and taking a flying leap on to the boat as it was three yards from the shore. "By jove, that was a near thing," he panted breathlessly. "Why, we're just coming in!" replied John.

Left to right – Jim Sharpe, Jos Hartley and Jack Bowman taken in the 1950s.

Late Charlotte Kipling

Another long serving ferryman was James Coward of Sawrey. He was born in Cunsey. He served on the ferry for 48 years and was never known to be late. He lived at the Post Office, in Sawrey, which was run by his wife. Mrs Coward's maiden name was Daft, and she was related to Richard Daft, a one time Captain of the England cricket team. James died in 1931.

Two other stalwarts were Jos Hartley (1928 - 1957) and Jack Bowman (1937 - 1972). The relief ferryman in their time was James W. Sharp who served from 1942 to at least 1954. In more recent times Mike Smith of Ambleside, Harold Gidman, Haslem Kellet and Dick Harrison were other well-remembered operators.

Jos Hartley was particularly noted for his exploits in other fields. His Aunt, Pol Hartley, held the licence of the Brown Horse at Winster, and Jos helped to manage the pub. He was involved in the construction of a Flying Flea, a tiny kit built aircraft powered by a British Anzani engine. Jos's machine is reputed to have made short flights but was never flown extensively. The type made its debut at the Paris Air Show in 1934, but by 1936 there had been so many fatalities it was grounded by the Authorities. While Jos lived at the Brown Horse there was a problem when another ferryman, who lived at Cunsey (possibly called Marshall) and Jos had to make arrangements for the boat to be left at the right side of the lake for whoever was on duty next morning. Reputedly they arranged to send the boat on its last trip without a driver! The boiler fire was allowed to die down, so that only sufficient steam pressure remained for one crossing. The ferry was sent across pilotless to ground gently and await the next morning's shift.

Jack Bowman served for over 35 years, but spent time in the Navy during the war, when he took part in Arctic convoys. He later claimed this experience was good training for some winter night crossings on the Ferry, particularly the bad winter of 1962/63 when the boat had to keep sailing through the night to avoid the ferry track freezing over. Early in his career he had a similar experience to John Atkinson, involving capricious animals. A drove of about seventy ponies was suddenly brought onto the boat, and not wanting to be ground down, he dashed into the cabin and shut the door. To the annoyance of the owners, the ponies clattered across the deck and fell into the water. The farmers, whose ponies they were, were not best pleased. Jack should have looped a chain across the exit ramp. Jack took a keen interest in sport, and the present author well remembers being chastised each Monday morning on his way to work at Ferry House, for his poor performance on the rugby field the previous Saturday.

The late Charlotte Kipling, who also worked at Ferry House, recalled several incidents which demonstrate the wholesome integration these men had in the social fabric of the district. She remembered Jos saying to her one day, "There's one who doesn't pay his fare." Charlotte had a Lakeland Terrier, called Vic, which sometimes accompanied her to work. Jos explained that the dog sometimes came down by himself, crossed on the Ferry, spent a couple of hours rabbiting, and then returned. Jack Bowman took a liking to another dog she had, and if it was with her, he would put the Ferry on slow to allow himself time to play with the dog. She was grateful on one occasion when having driven onto the Ferry, she discovered a tyre was flat. Jack got everyone to help and the wheel was changed by the time the crossing was complete. Jack was not averse to taking produce in kind in lieu of the fare.

A sad incident occurred in 1968 when the ferryman in charge was Dick Harrison. He suffered a heart attack while crossing, and with the boat at the Ferry House side the ambulance was called from Kendal. It had to go round the lake via Ambleside, and would have had to return the same way. To save time it was agreed that Ian Slater, then in his

Jack Gregg, from Ambleside, busy at work in the 1960s.
David & Irene Woodhouse (his daughter)

teens, whose parents both worked at Ferry House and who lived in accommodation over the adjacent garages, should drive the boat across. Ian went daily to school in Windermere and was familiar with the driving procedure. A story developed that because Mr Harrison died in mid-lake it was not known in which county his death should be registered (at that time the west shore of the lake was in Lancashire and the east in Westmorland). This was not the case and his death was registered in Westmorland.

The men who drive the Ferry and collect fares are only part of the team who keep the service running. The ongoing operation and maintenance involves a number of people in the background including office staff. One dedicated team's contribution was described in Cumbria Magazine in 1964. At that time the ferry 'Drake' was painted overall every two years. The activity took about two weeks depending on the weather, and was carried out while the boat was still operating. Joe Mallinson and Jack Gregg both had more than thirty years' Council service each, and usually spent their time painting road signs and markings. They scraped, cleaned, painted and varnished both inside and outside. In their two weeks' stint they would cross and recross the lake about six hundred times.

The Old Ferry Inn showing the Coat House clearly on the right.
Late Charlotte Kipling

Chapter Six

THE FERRY LANDINGS

The successful operation of the Windermere Ferry has been assisted by fortunately placed promontories sticking out opposite each other on the east and west shores, and almost equidistant from each end of the ten and a half mile long lake.

The work of landing and taking on horses, vehicles and people requires a suitable shore which is sufficiently stable to receive the landing ramps, has a shelving approach with sufficient depth of water to allow easy beaching, and with adjacent protection for waiting passengers.

THE WEST LANDING — FERRY HOUSE

The West Landing at Ferry House has added interest because a range of activities linked with its location have occurred over the centuries. The promontory on which the West Landing is located has been known by various names. An early name was Swines Ness, but the origin of this name is now lost. James Clark's map of 1789 shows the promontory to be called Great Boat and the area where it joins the mainland as Lamb's Gate. The bay behind the promontory is now called Mitchell's Wyke.

From at least the early 18th century an inn stood close to the lakeshore, by the ferry landing. Mention is made in an indenture of 1707 of a 'Coat for passengers,' which was probably a waiting room, though when it was rebuilt in 1789 the contract stated it should be 32 feet by 17 feet by 10 feet high and should be fit for the running of carriages into the coathouse. On early prints showing the Ferry Inn, a wide-open doorway of these proportions can be seen in the facade of the building, adjacent to the ferry landing.

The Ferry Inn was a noted centre for wrestling, sports and regattas. Between 1811 and 1861 regular events took place on the bowling green, the site of the present Ferry House. A notice in the Westmorland

Gazette for 8th August 1820 lists the events and prize money for the Annual Regatta on Windermere at Ferry House.

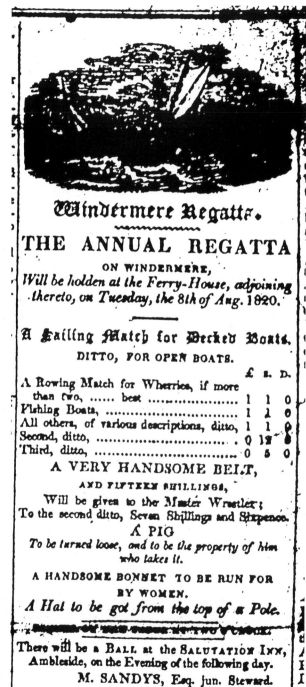

Copy of notice of the Regatta in the Westmorland Gazette – 5th August 1820. *Local Studies Section, Kendal Library*

Etching of Ferry House, Regatta, Windermere
Lake by T Allom and J Starling.

The Westmorland Gazette on 12th August 1820 (the following week) reports:

'On account of the extreme wetness of the day on Tuesday last, the Regatta on Windermere was very thinly attended. There was little or no sailing, and some of the prizes were not contended for'
(So what is new! - Author)

Underneath this article follows a social tit bit:

'The Ball, at Ambleside, on Wednesday evening, was remarkably well attended. Dancing commenced at nine o'clock. Miles Sandys, Esq. and Miss C. Watson, opened the Ball. The company did not separate until a late hour.'

Ellen Weeton in her Journal of a Governess in April 1810 gave an amusing description of a regatta she attended.

'After a rowing match or two, which began the entertainment, there followed a footrace by four men. Two of them ran without shirts; one had breeches on, the other only drawers... Expecting they would burst or come off, the ladies durst not view the race, and turned away from the sight. And well it was they did, for during the race, and with the exertion of running, the drawers actually did

Regatta and boat race engraving by T Unwins (undated). Though clearly on a better day! *Local Studies, Kendal Library*

burst, and the man cried out as he run – 'O Lord! O Lord! I cannot keep my
tackle in, G-d d-n it! I cannot keep my tackle in.'
The ladies, disgusted, every one left the ground; there were many of fashion and
rank; amongst others, Lady Diana Fleming, and her daughter Lady Fleming,
the Bishop of Llandaff's daughter; several carriages, barouches[1], curricles[2]; but
all trooped off.'

The Ferry Ring was the principal wrestling place in the district in the early 19th century. However, it was gradually replaced by other events and was completely supplanted by the Grasmere Sports after 1861. The Ferry Sports were visited in 1857 by Charles Dickens and his friend Wilkie Collins. The day after the Sports, Dickens even tried a fall with Thomas Longmire, the champion wrestler of his time at the New Hall Inn, Bowness. John Wilson of Elleray was a noted supporter. Wilson lived in Windermere, and was Professor of Moral Philosophy at Edinburgh University. He also edited Blackwood's Magazine and used the pen name of Christopher North. Professor Wilson encouraged the Sports and Regatta. He presented wrestling belts, and it is thought that the event at Ferry House began to lose support after his death in 1854.

Wilson had a particular liking for the Ferry, and his biographer states that every Saturday at least he would go down to the Ferry and steer the heavily laden boat across. Since the boat would have been propelled and steered with the oars this means he must have taken his turn at the sweeps. Wilson was an athletic man and this chance for activity was probably relished. On one crossing a splashing was seen in the water and on investigation they captured a large fish with two tails. It turned out to be a monster pike, which had tried to swallow a smaller one.

Among other activities at Ferry House, Cowper describes a Cherry Fair. This appears to have been a free invitation to all to gather fruit from a clump of fine, wild cherry trees, during two or three consecutive Sundays or the cherry season. He compared it to the Martindale Cherry Sunday and Longwathby Plum Sunday.

Prior to the introduction of a steam ferry in 1870 the landing itself, judging by prints of the time, was a wide stretch of shore covered in small stones. A prominent raised wooden structure was present, which passing sailing boats and the early steamers presumably used. The ferry itself is shown grounded at different points along the landing. The

1 Barouche - an open 4-wheeled carriage similar to those used by the Queen on state occasions.
2 Curricle - a 2-wheeled gig with a folding hood.

advent of the steam ferry, which used a chain and later cables, meant that a single landing point was necessary. This would have necessitated a permanent attachment of some strength. The landing point would also have needed a more stable basis, to allow firm grounding of the ramp and the subsequent passage of carriage wheels and horses' hooves at the same point. The style of this arrangement can be seen on early postcards and photographs.

From 1920 the Lancashire and Westmorland Joint Ferry Committee operated the Ferry. The Committee minutes record numerous problems with the maintenance of the landings. Inclement weather and abnormal lake levels caused most of them. In 1935 it was noted that the service had to be stopped two or three times a year on account of floods. In 1939 it was recorded that there had been considerable interference with normal running owing to floods and high winds. Most serious of these occurrences was on the occasion of the exceptional flood of July 30th and 31st, when the lake level rose five feet above normal level. All vehicular traffic was stopped between about 8.15 am on the 30th until 4 pm on the 31st, when with the help of Mr Bruce Dixon of Hawkshead, Sawrey (Timber Merchant) who obtained about fifty timber logs and also by making use of timber from the County Council's quarries, ramps were formed to enable vehicles to get on the boat. Ramps were kept in position until August 4th, but fluctuations in water level necessitated their frequent attention.

Accidents on the landings occasioned by users not realising the boat had left or was just arriving caused concern. In 1959 the Clerk reported a claim made by a motorist in respect of an accident which had occurred to his car by driving down to the water's edge after the boat had left the landing. It was resolved to place notices indicating that vehicles and persons must not be driven or walk on the ramps when the boat is moving. This measure did not prove adequate, and in 1960 following another accident, lifting barriers were provided on the boat's ramps at a cost of £520.

The Ferry Inn deserves a book in its own right. Apart from the sporting and social events already mentioned, the Inn itself always had a good reputation for food and accommodation. Its location alone, with outstanding views up and down the lake, is lauded in numerous guidebooks. The original Inn stood close to the water's edge shaded by a group of seven sycamore trees, which appear prominently in many illustrations. (Cowper noted that a red kite nested in these trees until 1790). Writing in 1842, Professor Wilson extolled the virtues of the Inn, claim-

South entrance to the Ferry Hotel in the 1920s.   *The RAP Co Ltd, London*

ing there was not a prettier place on all Windermere than the Ferry House, or one better adapted for a honeymoon.

> *'You can hand your bride into a boat almost out of the parlour window, and be off among the islands in a moment, or into nook or bay where no prying eye, even through a telescope (a most unwarrantable instrument), can overlook your happiness.'*

The old inn was demolished in 1879 and was replaced by the present building constructed by Pattinsons of Windermere. George Harry Pattinson described the building of the new hotel by his grandfather, G. Henry Pattinson in 1880-81. The old inn was pulled down and the new building was erected on the site of the old wrestling ring. Mr Pattinson records that:

> *'The new hotel had to have cellars, but excavation was impossible due to lake levels, so an ingenious plan was devised. The ground floor was designed and built as cellars, and then thousands of carts of soil were banked up around it so that the first floor became the ground floor and the cellars were 'underground'. He continues, 'The new hotel was started in 1880 and completed in time for the 1881 season. The winter of 1880-81 was one of great frost and Windermere was frozen over. This enabled timber for the hotel to be brought across the ice, dragged by men on skates. I was interested in some re-skimming of ceilings there which we (i.e. Pattinsons) did in about 1949. When our plas-*

Inglenook in the lounge of the Ferry Hotel.   *The RAP Co Ltd, London*

> *terer was asked why the skimming had come off, he said the work had been done in a frosty time, and pointed out the frost markings on the undercoat.'*

Mr Pattinson did not comment on the fact it had nevertheless stayed up nearly 70 years! His grandfather's brother Joseph designed the new hotel.

From local directories the following people are identified as licensees.

1829	WM GASKIN
1834	THOMAS CLOUSDALE
1848	BENJAMIN BILLS
1851	JAMES ARNOLD
1866	DANIEL TURNER
1869	RICHARD HOWE
1882	BRUCE LOGAN (FIRST TENANT OF THE NEW HOTEL)
1920	COLONEL MARSHALL AND MR SANDILANDS
1930	MR AND MRS STANLEY

In 1948 the hotel was offered for sale and was bought to become the Windermere Headquarters of the Freshwater Biological Association at a cost of £23,000. The Ferry rights were subsequently sold to the Lancashire and Westmorland County Councils for £5000.

Steamer Pier and view from the front of the Ferry Hotel.   *The RAP Co Ltd, London*

Advertising what the Hotel has to offer together with the tariff for staying.
Late Eric Clark

73

Splendid view of a yacht race in front of Ferry Hotel in the 1890s.
Pictorial Stationery Co Ltd, London

The Ferry House, now the Headquarters of the Freshwater Biological Association.

THE EAST LANDING — FERRY NAB

The East Landing at Ferry Nab has a less extensive repertoire of interest. James Clark in his Survey of the Lakes in 1789, shows three landings close together but at different angles. Presumably these allowed an appropriate approach depending on the wind direction. Clark's maps show the two basins of Windermere (north and south) on separate charts. The Ferry, being in the middle, appears on both. Sadly the depiction of the ferry boat landings on the two charts differ - the northern one showing a Y shaped landing, and the southern one three separate landings. Later photographs and maps confirm the presence of well-constructed stone flagged landings, which would have allowed the boat to approach from different angles. The introduction of the cable driven steam ferry would have allowed them to fall into disuse and become overgrown. They can now only be seen with difficulty.

A row of old cottages (now demolished) on the approach to the Nab was traditionally available as accommodation for ferrymen. A record in the Joint Ferry Committee minutes for 1957 shows that when Ferryman Jos Hartley died, the Committee agreed that his widow could continue to live in Ferry Cottage. Pictures of the landing through the 1900s show a wooden hut, used for passenger shelter, and a bunker for coal, when the ferry was steam driven.

Two hundred years later (9th November 1989) very little can be seen of the landing.

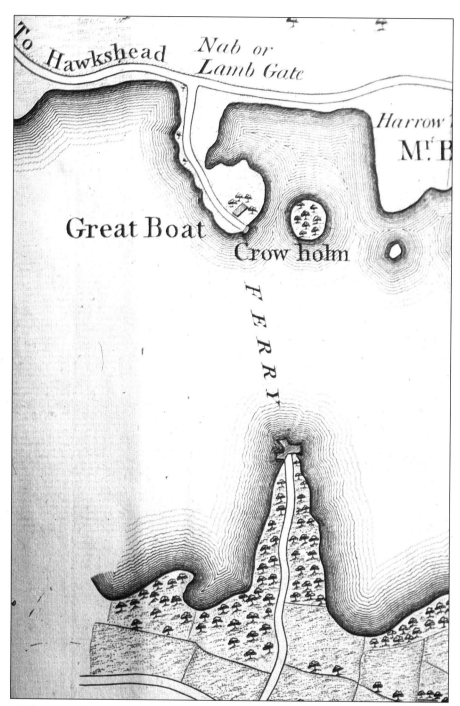

Clark's Map of 1789 showing the three landings.

Early photograph of Main Road, Windermere in the late 19th early 20th century.
John Marsh Collection

Stengal photograph of a different view of Main Road, Windermere.
John Marsh Collection

Abraham's of Keswick photograph of St Martin's Square, Bowness.

The Promenade, Bowness, showing the roadway full of people.

Chapter Seven

FROZEN LAKE

In some winters Windermere freezes over. Sometimes only partly, but in a number of years e.g. 1895, 1929, 1946 and 1963 it has been frozen from end to end. These occasions are memorable. Hundreds of skaters enjoy the opportunity to cross the lake on ice, or skate uninterruptedly for several miles. Ice yachts were common, and even horses and carriages were driven over the frozen lake. In 1963 Ferry House staff went to work over the ice on motor and pedal cycles. Keeping the ferry track clear of ice was not popular with skaters! It prevented them achieving an end-to-end skate of the lake, as they had to leave the ice and rejoin it again round the end of the clear track.

Such freezes cause problems for the Ferry. In some cases it has been necessary for the boat to be kept moving hourly through the night to keep the ferry track clear. As recently as the early 90s ferryman Arthur Wilson recalls his first crossing taking much longer than usual as he went slowly across allowing the cables to lift and split the ice.

In the poem, 'The Minstrels of Winandermere,' by Charles Farish written in 1811, several verses describe how the then ferryman dealt with the problem.

> *The great boat shall be heard to go*
> *Thro' the cold night from shore to shore,*
> *While freezing ice and melting snow*
> *Press heavy on the restless oar.*
> *Nor yet the boatman's task be done,-*
> *He dips his hands into the tide,*
> *And heaves huge ice-boards, one by one,*
> *Heaping a wall on either side;*
> *Winning his way across the lake,*
> *With battering maul and iron crow;*
> *The ice still closing in his wake,*

The 'Drake' crossing the frozen lake 1962-63 and keeping the ferry track ice free.
The late Charlotte Kipling

Lake showing 1890s freeze – note the amount of people on the lake and the ice yacht on the left. Pictorial Stationery Co Ltd, London.

In one the knitting fragments grow.
And when these arts will serve no more,
With hawser and with rustic sleight
He slides the pondrous boat ashore;
The kneeling camel ships her freight.

Late 1920s picture showing people just enjoying the walk on the ice.
Courtesy of the Margaret Duff Collection

Steve Phelps on duty in the Lake Warden's Boat in 1996 with the Ferry in the
background. *Courtesy of the Lake Warden's Office*

PC Bob Crowther in the Police Boat Vigilant IV in late 1980s with Cunsey in the
background. *Courtesy of Bob Crowther*

Chapter Eight

LAKE WARDENS AND POLICE

As the lake traffic increased through the 1960s, it was found necessary to provide patrol and rescue boats on the lake. A Lake Warden was appointed and provided with a suitable boat to administer the local authority's regulations. Later the police too operated a launch to maintain law and order. During their operations they had to deal with a number of ferry related incidents. Among those involved were policemen Jack Little, Bob Crowther, John Makin, Ken Thwaites, John Norton, Bob Yates, Alan Pattinson, Neil Thompson and Paul Latham who served at different times on the police launch. Jim Maguire, Philip Markland, Tommy Moss, George Dixon, Roger Quartermaine and Mike Nield were among those who acted as Lake Wardens. Windermere Urban District Council who appointed Bert Lake in 1947 started an early version of the Lake Warden Service.

The Lake Windermere Byelaws specifically identify the Ferry and lay down conditions for it:

4.13 The Windermere Ferry shall carry headlights in its direction of motion, together with deck illumination.

6.14 All vessels shall, whenever possible, pass astern of the Windermere Ferry. Whether passing astern or ahead, vessels shall not pass nearer than two ferry lengths (60 metres) of the said ferry except that no vessel shall pass between the said ferry and the shore when the said ferry is within three ferry lengths (90 metres) of the shore.

Some examples of the incidents they dealt with show the variety of problems that arose. In the early 90s a youth from Liverpool realised that the cash taken as fares on the Ferry was kept in the wheelhouse in the upper cabin. Seizing an opportunity when the crew was occupied on the car deck, he attempted to steal the money from the till, but was observed. Calmly the ferryman stopped the boat in mid-lake, and called for police assistance on his radio. PC Bob Crowther was attending a canoe race at Fell Foot (near the bottom of the lake about four miles away). He made best speed to the Ferry and after some twenty minutes came quickly alongside. He boarded the stationary ferry and apprehended the villain. The passengers were beginning to be concerned, but the incident was over before a lynching mob could form! No one profited, as the thief threw his loot into the lake.

The Police Boat attended several incidents in which cars ran out of control down the landing ramps and into the lake. Most were pulled out without damage, and even started despite the wetting. A Robin Reliant was less fortunate and became crushed under the ramp. A Volkswagen floated as it entered the water, but sank when the occupants opened the windows to escape. The local bobbies seemed most amused when a south country off duty policeman on a BMW motorcycle drove off the ferry ramp at Ferry Nab on a wet and windy evening and landed unceremoniously and embarrassingly in the lake, the Ferry at this time was at Ferry House. When asked what had happened the dripping wet pillion passenger simply said he had seen the sign, 'Ferry 20 minutes,' and thought 'we've a long way to go yet,' and the next thing he knew he was up to his neck in water! The motorcycle had gone so far into the water that it had gone off the edge of the ferry ramp and despite best efforts could not be lifted back on shore that night and had to remain underwater with its headlight on until morning!

Serious accidents have been avoided, no fatalities or serious injuries being recorded in recent years. Minor scrapes were dealt with as road traffic accidents, since technically the Ferry is regarded as a floating bridge and is part of the highway. One embarrassed driver locked himself out of his car when it was on the Ferry and he journeyed backwards and forwards about ten times until the police opened the car.

The ferrymen had occasional navigation problems with other boats. On one occasion a speedboat, which had just undergone do it yourself repairs had came dangerously close, and the warning hooter was sounded. Sadly, when the speedboat driver threw open his throttle and turned his wheel to take avoiding action, he found the repair work had reversed his controls and the speedboat ended up on the Ferry's landing ramp. At another time, a resident houseboat owner, known for his contempt for navigational niceties, came too close and was lifted out of the water on the Ferry's cables. When asked why they had collided the Ferry crew stated, "Because he didn't move!"

Road sign warning unsuspecting motorists of ferry landing.

For the most part there were harmonious relations between the Ferry and the police. Relations did become strained on one occasion when a local Councillor objected after he discovered that police cars crossing on the Ferry did not pay a fare.

William Wordsworth by
Abraham's of Keswick.
Anne Bonney

John Ruskin at Brantwood by
Abraham's of Keswick.
John Marsh Collection

Chapter Nine

PASSENGERS

It is not possible to estimate how many people have crossed on the Ferry boats over the centuries. Most would be ordinary people going about their business. Some were more noteworthy, though this does not mean their impressions are any more valuable.

THOMAS GRAY (1716-71)

The poet Thomas Gray used the Ferry whilst on a tour of the Lakes. The following account has survived.

'As I am aware of the curiosity which most persons have to know any small particulars of the life of an eminent man, I shall here insert a genuine anecdote of Mr Gray. This gentleman who was no less remarkable for his timidity than his poetry, went (by land) to Bowness. Here he was told that the best point of view was on the opposite shore, a little above Nab Gate. Curiosity and a bore for natural beauties, were strong incitements on the one hand, but the reflection that there was no convenient way of attaining his desire, unless by crossing the lake in a boat was a reason almost equally strong for staying where he was. Being told however that not only horses and carriages frequently were ferried over there, but that the common carrier from Kendal to Hawkshead used that conveyance he ventured to set forward blindfolded. He was accordingly landed near Nab Gate, had viewed the landscape and taken out his mirror in order to view it in miniature, when he saw the boat returning for more passengers; then asking his guide if any persons had ever been lost in crossing the Ferry? The guide told him that about the year 1635 forty-seven passengers were lost, owing to their own imprudence by oversetting the boat as they were returning from Hawkshead fair.'

'This at once determined Mr Gray not to embark a second time and he accordingly began to look about for some road to take him to Bowness by land. Lifting up his eyes he saw impending precipices on every side (except the lake), *a sight as alarming to him as a second voyage; he was so agitated at the prospect, that he trembled for fear, and had just command enough of himself to say to his guide, "get me to Bowness any way;" nor did he utter another word, or even look up, till he arrived there. He then set off immediately for Kendal but has in his account of his tour entirely suppressed every hint of this curious journey.'*

WILLIAM WORDSWORTH (1770-1850)

The Lakeland poet went to school in Hawkshead and his love of the surrounding countryside and people is often seen in his poetry. In 1788 William returned to Hawkshead for his first summer vacation from Cambridge. He was particularly pleased to see again the old ferryman on Windermere, one who had taken him across the lake so many times over the years, going back and forth to school.

William's friendship with the ferryman is recorded in the Prelude, IV. 5-9 (1805):

> *I bounded down the hill, shouting amain*
> *A lusty summons to the farther shore*
> *For the old Ferryman; and when he came*
> *I did not step into the well known boat*
> *Without a cordial welcome.*

William's sister Dorothy recorded in her Journal on 8th June 1802, 'crossed the lake with our horse in the Ferry.'

REV'D CHARLES FARISH (1766-?)

Charles Farish was the First Assistant at Hawkshead School in Wordsworth's time. He is known for his poem 'The Minstrels of Winandermere', which centres on two crossings of the Ferry at Bowness, involving nine schoolboys, the ferryman George Robinson and his daughter Edith who composed songs about the district.

T.W. Thompson in his 'Wordsworth's Hawkshead' recounts a visit made to the Ferry, by Farish.

'On their arrival at Great Boat early in the morning George, the ferryman, unmoored the smaller of the ferry-boats, the more suitable for landing them 'far in Bowness Bay'; his daughter Edith brought them their 'ready breakfast', milk

warm from the cows. We learn of George's delight in 'woody Crowholme' which was the island nearest to his house; an island that, like Ferry Nab, was part of the Great Boat estate, as it existed in the eighteenth century. The boys embarked, one taking the helm another an oar, while a third 'the fishing tackle flings.' George landed them at Bowness.

At night long after sunset, they made their way to 'Bowness Point, which is Farish's name for Ferry Nab and called loudly for George. On the Point there was a ruined smithy that afforded shelter from the wind; and the Hawkshead carrier, arriving from Kendal told them he had drunk many a stoup of ale in 'this same blacksmith's castle.' There were other arrivals, early and late, including one or two more men with horses and carts, it appears. Then came George, who with 'measur'd oar' had rowed his ponderous boat across the lake, guided to the Nab he sought by a lantern he kept burning there at night near to the ruined smithy. He came ashore and trimmed it carefully, whilst he did so the boys helped to wheel the carts aboard, the horses having been loosed from the shafts for the crossing. George told them that once on a stormy night, when his 'little lighthouse was buried under snow, the flame had not gone out. On the return journey he was guided to the mooring by his daughter Edith, to whom his usual signal was the raising of a light on board his boat accompanied by a loud hail; and Farish pictures her coming with 'cheerful haste' to the Great-Boat-tree, a light in her hand, her fluttering apron extended round the flame rashly but with skill. Her father said that when the mist was thick and black he had sometimes got her to keep on calling, and had shaped his course by her voice alone. We hear something, too, of his labours when the lake was frozen in its shallower parts; of how 'with battering maul and iron crow' he broke a way across, heaving with his hands the 'huge ice-boards' to either side, only to see them knit together again in his wake; and how, when the ice defeated him, he slid his massive boat ashore with hawser and rustic sleigh.'

JOHN RUSKIN (1819-1900)

Ruskin, was an eminent Victorian, known for his art criticism and support for the arts and crafts movement. He lived the last part of his life at Brantwood on Coniston Water. He had visited the Lakes all his life and published several accounts of his visits.

In his diary for 1830 Ruskin mentions crossing the Ferry.

'6th July, Tuesday, Low Wood.
The next morning we proposed to go to Coniston and being informed there
would be no rain that day we accordingly set off for the place.
We proceeded about five miles when we reached the Ferry where there was a
large boat. The horses first entered and were first tied up at one end. The car-
riage was next with some difficulty rolled after them and last we followed. This
sail was not quite so agreeable as some others that we had had. However we got
over without any terrible misfortune and landed safely on the other side.'

There is a footnote accompanying the passage. "On this day, their route down the side of Windermere by carriage through Bowness to the Ferry would have followed the way they had rowed home from Bowness on the previous day. A ferry service had been operated at this, the narrowest point on Windermere, since 1454. In 1830 the ferry rights were owned by the Curwen family and the service was operated by the Ferry Inn. Until 1869 when the first steam ferry was introduced, the boats were large flat-bottomed craft operated by oars. In 'Iteriad' Ruskin wrote of the ferry:

'That the waters may not bar the path of the rover,
A kind of hobblety boat paddles over;
And, in order to urge on its clumsiness fast,
They've got a huge oar that might do for a mast:
And. what is much worse, they have not got a sail,
That might catch in its foldings the breath of a gale.'

Apparently the ferryman 'demanded and asked an exorbitant price,' and in order to avoid the Ferry and its high price, they returned by way of the main road through Skelwith Bridge and round the head of Windermere, to Ambleside and Low Wood, a distance of about ten miles."

A watercolour of the Ferry by William Gastineau is included in the 'Iteriad.' The painting was exhibited at Birmingham City Art Gallery in 1992, but it was identified as being of Loch Dhune, in Galloway. The painting was also reproduced in Country Life on 14th October 1976 where it was described as being of Mullion Cove in Cornwall! Ruskin would have been mortified.

MR FLEMING

An interesting cameo piece in the North Lonsdale Magazine (August 1899) describes a ferry crossing in Victorian times. A Mr Fleming was travelling to his 'cottage near a wood' in Hawkshead where he holidayed.

We drove quickly through Windermere and Bowness; then by a mile or so of winding road to the 'Nab', a tiny foreland on the eastern shore of Windermere lake. 'The boat is on the other side,' said our driver, and waved one of his lamps. We waited in the fast gathering darkness till a steam whistle from the Lancashire side told us that the horse ferry barge had started from Ferry, and in five minutes we heard the rattling of chains as the gangway was lowered. The horses fearlessly advanced, and in fifteen seconds we were settled on board, where we had a friendly smile from Isaac Brockbank, but he did not give the expected signal. We still lingered. 'What is it Isaac? Why can't we start?' 'Don't you hear the carrier? We must wait for him.' Sure enough in the near distance there was a rumble of slow heavy wheels, and the squeak of axles that would have been better for the oil can. So we listened to the gentle breaking of the ripples on the narrow strip of pebbly beach till, by the light of a hurricane lantern, we saw a clumsy looking wagon surmounted by huge hoops over which was stretched an awning of some heavy woollen stuff. Our carriage was moved a little forward and then there was room and to spare for 't'carrier's cart.' When we reached Ferry the darkness hid the inn, the graceful group of trees in front of it, and the beautifully wooded Claife Heights behind, which give a unique charm to this beautifully situated hotel.'

BEATRIX POTTER (1866-1943)

The children's author, best known for her Peter Rabbit, Jemima Puddleduck and Squirrel Nutkin books among others, lived at Far Sawrey for many years. She would have travelled often across the Ferry. In her Journal she recalls staying at the Ferry Hotel in September 1895 and she observed that '... it was reasonable in charge, cooking and attendance excellent but I thought the company more than usually disagreeable, and did not like it at all.' She particularly disliked the Yacht Club types who lounged about and led her to feel she would like to kick their shins.

Judy Taylor in her book, 'So Shall I tell You a Story,' about Beatrix, tells how she '... mounted a campaign to stop flying boats on Windermere. She wrote to Country Life complaining of probable 'danger, turmoil and possibly pecuniary damage .... at the hand of fellow man' to animals crossing on Windermere ferry in that 'ramshackle picturesque boat ... 'which might be caused by the noise of the propeller of the hydroplane.' Her campaign was entirely successful; it prompted a government inquiry and before the end of the year the planes had left Windermere.

ARTHUR RANSOME (1784-1967)

Ransome's Swallows and Amazons adventures which are set in a mixture of Coniston and Windermere locations might have had the Walker, Blackett and Callum children encountering the ferry on their various adventures. Disappointingly, Ransome seems to have ignored the potential of the boat. Captain John and Boy Roger could have used it to confirm their opinion that steamers are simply tin boxes with engines. Able Seaman Titty would, no doubt, have found a romantic explanation for its presence, perhaps a hospital ship or floating store. Dick Callum would surely have thrilled at the cable guides and driving wheel. Nancy and Peggy of course would have seen a valuable prize of war. Sadly it appears to have been ignored though Ransome himself doubtless crossed on the Ferry many times.

MOIRA HOUSE SCHOOL

In September 1940 the staff and pupils of Moira House Girls' School in Eastbourne were evacuated to the Ferry Hotel. Mary Gay Platt, Chairman of the present school council, and an old girl of the school, who was evacuated to Windermere, kindly provided some relevant extracts from 'The Shuttle,' the school magazine, and her own impressions of being at the Ferry Hotel and using the Ferry.

The school had started looking for a suitable emergency location in 1938 before the war started. After an initial temporary move to Devonshire, the school was very relieved to obtain a more suitable centre for the period of the emergency when the Ferry Hotel became available. While the Hotel provided most of the facilities such a school needed, playing fields could only be found in Bowness across the lake where tennis courts and games pitches were located.

The Ferry was their link with the rest of the world and is mentioned in the school magazine at regular intervals. Some excerpts include the following:

> 'Watching the Ferry boat or crossing on it is ever of interest, and especially so when it is crowded with figures in red caps, red shirts and blue tunics, lined up on each side of the cars down its centre. The men on the Ferry are always kind to us. They wait for us if we are a little late for games and sometimes even bring the Ferry back, if it has left the shore, without grumbling about it.'
> (December 1940)

When it came time to return to Eastbourne comments were made about how strange life would be

> '.....unregulated by a ferry whose service ends at 8.45 pm in winter and 9.45 pm in summer: a ferry that brings our 'daily bread', and our letters when the ferry-man thinks of it, and our coal, and our visitors; that makes our only link with games fields and railway station; and that three times yearly, in winter darkness or summer dawns, runs exclusively for us at 5.45 am, when after breakfast at 5.15, suitcase laden girls board it on their way to the 'School Special' that carries them miraculously from Windermere to Victoria.'
> (December 1944)

Mary Gay recalls being handed a penny for her fare when one of her sisters and her husband were meeting her on the other side of the lake one Sunday in spring 1941. In June 1941, the Joint Ferry Committee agreed to special terms for the girls when crossing and re-crossing to their recreational grounds in Bowness. After this the girls just said 'school' to the ferryman whether they were going to games or on shopping trips or bike rides at weekends, and went across free.

She remembers that the ferrymen were particularly good to them, letting the girls crowd round the boiler house to keep warm in winter. On one memorable occasion in January 1942 when the school train was thirteen hours late, they arrived in the early morning instead of the evening. The ferrymen stayed up all night and kept the Ferry ready for them. With no mobile phones or fax no one knew when this would be and the school kitchen changed the food from soup to porridge at about four in the morning so that they had something hot when they arrived. Mary Gayalso recalls that if anyone asked the time they looked out of the window to see where the Ferry was rather than looking at the clock. Mary Gay's older cousin, also at the school, recalled a 'real thrill', though rather unpatriotic, when two or three Luftwaffe officers were being ferried across to a prisoner of war camp (probably Grizedale Hall). The girls were warned not to look at them, and certainly not smile. The officers were smashing looking and their uniforms gorgeous. The older girls who looked quite unusually attractive in their red boys caps and short shorts, did have a little look, and a little smile, and may have cheered the poor men up a little bit!

Chapter Ten

THE CRIER OF CLAIFE

Many references are made by those who have written about the Ferry to the 'Crier of Claife'. Thompson records that the first appearances in print of this legend were by Harriet Martineau (1855) and by A. Craig Gibson in 'The Lakeland of Lancashire' (1867). Gibson's account is as follows:

> *It is said that, more than 300 years ago, the Ferry on Windermere was haunted by a troublesome night walker, crying in a manner that enforced attention, from the Westmoreland shore, for a boat; the most urgent and most awful appeals always coming on the most stormy nights. One of the ferrymen who attended to this weirdly hail when first heard, and rowed across the lake against a fierce gale from the south-east, returned with an empty boat, horror stricken and dumb, continuing speechless for some days and then dying. Travellers began to avoid the Ferry, for the crier continued to haunt the knab every stormy night; and 'over all there hung a cloud of fear,' so that few cared to venture near it even by day.*

The legend continues with the laying of the ghost in a quarry on Claife by monks from the island chapel on St Mary Holme.

Cowper believed the tale to be a modern invention, and found no confirmation of an incident that could have given rise to it. He was dismissive of it as having any foundation.

Hardwick D. Rawnsley, a noted literary figure and a founder of the National Trust, took the fable seriously enough to publish a poem about the Crier in his Sonnets at the English Lakes (1882) which is as follows:

The Criér of Claife
The priests who served at Sire de Courci's shrine
Might ply the ghost with candle, book and bell,
But that old Crier of Claife on Furness Fell,

As long as ivy evergreen shall twine,
May sally forth at will from his ravine,
And rouse the boatman with his human yell:
Winds are not laid by sacradotal spell,
And spirits own a Master more Divine.
Oft when the storm goes scurrying up the height
I hear the hollow moaning of the wind
Like ghosts in sorrow, and a word of Christ's
Linked with that monkish failure, fills the night :
"Can Mortals track the free wind home, or bind
The Spirit blowing ever as it lists?"

Chapter Eleven
FERRY FARES

For some years at the beginning of the last century, the steamboat 'Esperance' ran an alternative service from the Ferry Hotel to Bowness for foot passengers and cyclists. It ran every three quarters of an hour throughout the day. Recently a similar service has been restarted by Windermere Lake Cruises. It has been operating for two years and its timetable is co-ordinated with a bus service for onward connection to Sawrey and Hawkshead.

Windermere Ferry always seems to have been a pay ferry. The fare for a pedestrian in 1699 was 1d, and as can be seen from the table below, rose only gradually until the mid-20th century.

	1699	1830	1900	1928	1954	1968	1989	2001
FARE FOR A FOOT PASSENGER	1d	2d	2d Rtn	3d	3d	6d	10p	40p

In 1699 the then ferry operator Thomas Braithwaite wanted to increase the 1d fare. A document cited by Cowper, names Miles Sandys of Graythwaite, William Rawlinson of the same and Oliver Sands of Sawrey Infra[1], together with some forty-five residents of surrounding parishes on the Lancashire shore, and sets out the case against raising the fare. The signatories agree to pay the costs of any legal action. A flavour of the dispute can be gained from the wording of the first paragraph.

Witnesseth as followeth:
Whereas time out of mind itt hath beene ussed and Accustomed that the pties to these presents and all others who have had occasion ffrom time to time to passe repasse & travell over Windermer Watter Att the ffery boate on the Kings hyeway there have time beyond the memory of man ussed and Accustomed to

---

1 Far Sawrey was known as Extra, and Near Sawrey as Infra at that time.

The steam boat 'Esperance' waiting to take passengers to Bowness directly from the
Ferry Landing.   *Photochrom Co Ltd, London & Tunbridge Wells*

*pay only one penny and noe more ffor their soe passing & repassing or goeing
and rereturneing ouer the said ferry-boat to the ferryman in respect of his pay;
And now Thomas Braithwaite the ffery man there hauing Lately built a new
ffery boat Refuseth to receive the said Accustomed pay Intending to exact upon
us & other his maisties subjects in raiseing the accustomed pay of the said ferry.
In consideration whereof and to the intent a Legall tryall may be had with the
said Thomas Braithwt the fferyman in order to settle the Accustomed pay and
his Attendance upon the same att all times when any of his Maisties subjects
have occasion to use the said ffery boat the said Miles Sandys Willm
Rawlinson & Oliver Sands haue undertaken the care & burden to solicitt pros-
ecute & defend all such Actions either att Law or in Equity as shall bee neede-
ful to be brought prosecuted or defended from time to time concerning the
premisses.'*

The action appears to have been successful.

A different aspect of fare collection came into prominence in the
1920s when the running of the Ferry was taken over by Lancashire and
Westmorland Joint Ferry Committee. The previous operator, Mr Logan,
had relied on a perhaps less than efficient book-keeping system in relation to fares. The County Council's auditors were not impressed and
numerous entries in the Joint Ferry Committee's minutes throughout

Another view of the Esperance this time at Bowness, with the Old England on the left.
Pictorial Stationery Co Ltd, London

the twenties and early thirties make reference to the problem. The County Surveyor was asked to undertake the financial management of the Ferry and institute some form of ticket audit or checks on passenger numbers. In 1924 a periodical comparison of the number of tickets issued, with the cash accounted for, and a ticket stock book recording the number of tickets received from the printers, together with those issued and un-issued was adopted. Despite this, an entry in 1929 showed the auditors were still critical with regard to the collection of fares. In 1930 a secret check on ferry boat receipts had been carried out on eleven separate days and the Committee Chairman stated '... that in consequence of certain irregularities he had thought it advisable to take certain steps.' The Committee considered the matter in private. It was resolved that Mr Holt be appointed to collect all the takings from the Ferryman at 5 pm each day and pay the same into the bank regularly. In 1933 it was resolved that locks be fixed on the ticket boxes as suggested by the District Auditor, and that officials of the County Surveyor's and Accountant's staff be asked to visit the Ferry periodically for the purpose of verifying the number of passengers using the Ferry and comparing the result with the number of tickets shown to have been issued during the period of each visit. It is not difficult to conclude that the ferrymen of the time had considerably greater accountancy skills than the County Council staff!

In 1933 the Joint Ferry Committee dealt with a disputed charge

WINDERMERE FERRY SERVICE

Across Lake Windermere

Address: J Bowman Esq, 16 Victoria Street, WINDERMERE, Westmorland
Telephone: Windermere 1088

NOTE: *On ferries where passengers are allowed to remain in their vehicles, enough room must be left between vehicles for doors to be opened so that passengers could escape in an emergency.*

SERVICE: Daily every 15–20 minutes

Weekday—**Monday before Easter–September 15**
  7am–9.45pm
  September 16–Sunday before Easter
  7am–8.45pm

Sunday—As weekday but beginning at 10am

Bank Holidays—7am–10pm

Chris tmas Day—Sunday service

CAPACITY: 10 cars

TIME IN TRANSIT (pier to pier): 6 minutes

CHARGES (Owner's risk)

Vehicles (including driver)	Single		Day Return	
	s	d	s	d
Car up to 14ft	1	7	2	4
Car up to 20ft	2	4	3	10
Car over 20ft	4	8	7	0
Tri-car	1	3	1	3
Motor cycle with side-car	1	3	1	3
Motor cycle (solo)	1	0	1	0
Scooter	1	0	1	0
Motor caravan	As for cars			
Trailer caravan up to 14ft	1	7	2	4
Trailer caravan over 14ft	2	4	3	10
Passengers		6		6

when the owner of a four-seater 16hp Standard car registered number JA 1909 passed over the Ferry and refused to pay the proper fare of 2s 6d, but offered 1s 6d. The Clerk was instructed to trace the owner and take proceedings.

The owner of a motorcycle who held a contract for himself and machine complained of being charged if he did not bring his motor cycle.

The Committee had a human side. In 1940 they agreed that soldiers, sailors and airmen in uniform when using the Ferry on foot or with bicycles be charged half price. This concession was extended to women service personnel in 1941. The concession was withdrawn in 1946.

The Joint Ferry Committee could not alter the fares without approval from Whitehall, and in the Public Record Office at Kew there is a thick file containing correspondence annotated with civil servants' comments dealing with the Council's applications for increases. The content covers the period 1952 to 1957. Of particular interest is the section dealing with a proposed fare increase in 1956. The Council decided it needed a large price hike to pay the interest charges arising from the large sum that had been borrowed to pay for the new ferry 'Drake'. The Minister or rather his civil servants were not persuaded the rises were necessary, perhaps because they had been bombarded by complaints from local residents. Letters from landowners, parish councils and a two hundred and thirty-six name petition had put the cat among the pigeons. The author of this book was quite taken aback to find the original hand written petition in the file, and it included his own name together with many of those he worked with at Ferry House! The Minister appointed an Inspector to hold a Public Inquiry that took place in August 1956. The Inspector dismissed the complaints and approved the increases. However, the Inspector did recommend that the category of 'workman's ticket' was outdated (he said the term was Victorian) and everyone should be called simply 'a passenger.'

In more recent years fare disputes have centred on disproportionate increases in contract prices. In 1983 many residents became incensed about high fares, unreliable service and long queues of cars waiting for the boat. On Tuesday 31st May, a group of protesters drove their cars onto the Ferry, and for about two hours blockaded the service. Councillor, the late David Brayshaw, of Sawrey, who helped to organise the show of strength is reported to have said, "It has been a tremendous

Facing page: Price of travel on the Windermere Ferry in 1962

Ferry protesters showing their feelings in 1983. Fifth from right, Hilary Ainsworth and second from right is Mike Nield.   *Hilary Ainsworth*

success. We have got all these people here to support the campaign, just following a scratch meeting. We could have stayed all day, as we are allowed an unlimited number of journeys with our contract, but it would go sour. We have blocked it for nearly two hours, and that is enough."

Concerns resurfaced in 1995 when Cumbria County Council introduced a controversial new pricing policy. This time it was resolved by debate without the need for direct action. Interestingly the arena has changed over the centuries from local conflict involving residents, ferry owners and users, to the County Council and distant politicians in Carlisle.

Chapter Twelve
WINDERMERE FERRY TODAY

Arthur Wilson has been a ferryman for fifteen years. Previously he had been a long distance driver, specialising in moving racehorses. Following a broken back received in a riding accident, which left him immobile for six months, he had to give up driving. Hearing of a vacancy on the Ferry, he helped out for a week, and then stayed on. He enjoyed the work and meeting people, and the arrangements suited him well. Arthur now shares the principal duties with Chris Blezzard and Peter Goodlad, and there are other relief crew including Sean Arnott, Steve Harrison, Stewart Wilson and Richard Bland.

In his years travelling backwards and forwards across the lake Arthur recalls having talked with several celebrities, including: Stan Boardman, Eric Pollard, Jasper Carrot, Des Lynam and Bill Beaumont among many other TV and sporting personalities. He recalled with amusement the arrival of a film crew at 5am one morning to make an advertisement for a car. Helicopters zoomed in to take their shots, but after it was over the car would not start and it had to be manhandled off the Ferry. On another occasion a pop group used the boat as a location for filming a video.

One of his most dramatic experiences occurred one Saturday after-noon about 3pm, when he noticed a purplish-blue dark cloud gathering over Claife Heights. The Ferry was about in the middle of the lake when a mini tornado suddenly struck. The wind speed, measured on the boats anemometer touched 80 mph. Boats were turned over, trees were felled, waterspouts blew off the lake. The life rafts on the Ferry's cabin roof were blown away. Arthur advised his passengers to stay in their cars and foot passengers to shelter in the cabin. The storm passed quickly, but it was a frightening event.

There have been deaths from heart attack, requests for cremation ashes to be scattered on the lake and recently a lady told him that she had given birth in an ambulance while it was crossing on the Ferry. The

Arthur Wilson with his daughter Anna and his prize
winning marrow.   *Courtesy of the Westmorland Gazette*

ferrymen feel some satisfaction that on a number of occasions they had
been able to help the police. Indeed only a few days earlier a girl passenger had reported a wallet stolen, and by judicious control of the
Ferry's speed, the police were waiting at the landing and interviewed all
the passengers. The wallet was found hidden behind a display panel. At
another time they had noticed a golden coloured Vauxhall the police
had been looking for. Again the police were waiting at the landing and
an offender wanted in six counties was apprehended. Arthur was
intrigued on another occasion when a car ran forward off the landing
into the water. The male driver was adamant he didn't want the police
called. Arthur assumed the lady passenger did not want to be identified!

Unusual loads have included a coach and four horses, once common
place, they created quite a stir. Quite how a forty-foot long articulated
truck that arrived at the Ferry House side and found itself unable to
turn round was dealt with has to be left to the imagination. Exceeding

Peter Goodlad at the controls of the Mallard on 22nd January 2002.

Steven Harris who was in charge of loading the ferry and taking fares.

Road signs you see when approaching the ferry from Sawrey.

Mallard on 22nd January 2002 approaching Ferry House side.

the Ferry's maximum load it should not have been carried. Ferrymen are nothing if not obliging and resourceful!

Arthur who lives in Underbarrow, near Kendal, is proud of the fact that he has been responsible for encouraging an inter-village marrow competition. Underbarrow and Sawrey compete annually and the idea probably sprang from conversations while crossing on the Ferry. Marrows of eighty pounds or more in weight feature in the event. He also enjoys enlivening crossings by announcing over the public address system, when the boat is about to leave, that passengers should fasten their seat belts and extinguish their cigarettes.

Regular travellers on the Ferry regard the boat with a mixture of pleasure, nonchalance and irritation. The service provides an essential link and while for many it is just a fact of life, others enjoy the brief respite from everyday problems on their ten minute daily 'cruise'. They also enjoy the chance to chat with others and exchange news. For others who just miss the boat a twenty minute wait has to be endured. More serious irritation comes mainly from those occasions when adverse weather causes the service to be cancelled and an unexpected lengthy journey round the head of the lake results. Automatic signs at strategic places on the approach roads give warning when the service is suspended. The signs are activated by telephone from the ferry itself.

At busy times the waiting queues of cars can extend for many hundreds of yards and waits of an hour or more can be experienced. One passenger recalled that he had been waiting for the Ferry one day in his car, fell asleep and woke to see he had missed the boat. A Sawrey hotelier tells that collecting guests who cross on foot can be a problem, as their time of arrival is difficult to predict. Ferry cancellations also cause problems for the pubs that depend on regular deliveries. Every five years the Ferry has to be removed to the lakeside slipway for Lloyd's inspections and major overhaul. During this extended stoppage a launch provides a passenger service but vehicles must go round the lake. A few residents believe the Ferry has a hidden benefit as it regulates the amount of traffic that visits Sawrey, Claife and Cunsey and thus preserves the quiet peacefulness of the area.

What cannot be in doubt is that the Windermere Ferry is a venerable institution that has survived over the centuries and has provided a rich tapestry of people and events equal to anything seen elsewhere in the Lake District.

Cars alighting from the ferry on arrival on the Ferry House side.

Windermere Ferry Ticket – which allows you to take this delightful journey through time!

SOURCES

Armitt, M.L.: The Church of Grasmere: A history. Titus Wilson, Kendal. 1912.

Bicknell, P.: The Picturesque Scenery of the Lake District. St Paul's Bibliographies. 1990.

Braithwaite, G.E.: The Braithwaite Clan. L Tilley and son, Ledbury. Undated.

Clark, J.: A Survey of the Lakes of Cumberland, Westmorland and Lancashire. London 1789.

Collingwood, W.G.: 'The Fatal Nuptiall.' Transactions of the Cumberland and Westmorland Antiquarian and Archaeological Society, volume 13 NS.

County Record Office, Kendal: WC/S, records deposited by the County Surveyor. 7.6.1978.

County Record Office, Preston: The Graythwaite Papers (DDSa/)

County Record Office, Whitehaven: The Curwen Papers (D/Cu/)

Cowper, H S: Hawkshead. Bemrose and Sons, London. 1899.

Davies, H: William Wordsworth. Sutton Publishing 1997.

Dearden, J.S. (ed): A Tour of the Lakes in Cumbria – John Ruskin's diary for 1830. Scolar Press 1990.

Kipling, C.: The Commercial Fisheries of Windermere. Transactions of the Cumberland and Westmorland Antiquarian and Archaeological Society (TCWAAS) 72 NS.

Lindop, G.: A Literary Guide to the Lake District. Chatto and Windus. 1993.

North Lonsdale Magazine, volume 3, August 1899.

Pattinson, G.H.: The Great Age of Steam on Windermere. The Windermere Nautical Trust. 1981.

Pattinson, Private papers – kind permission of Diana Matthews.

Robertson, E.: Wordworthshire. Chatto and Windus. 1911.

Taylor, J. (ed): So Shall I Tell You A Story. Frederick Warne. 1993.

Thompson, B.L.: The Windermere Ferry: An Antiquarian Essay. Titus Wilson, Kendal. 1971.

Thompson, T.W.: Wordsworth's Hawkshead, edited by Robert Woof. OUP. 1970.

Weir, M.: Ferries in Scotland. John Donald. 1988.

White, W.: Furness Folk and Facts, Titus Wilson, Kendal. 1930.

Wood, B.: Ferries and Ferrymen. Cassel. 1969.